LUIZ BIRMAN

DEBIT CARD

The emotional side of money and credit

UNDERLINE
PUBLISHING

ISBN 978-1-962185-89-9

Published by Underline Publishing LLC.
www.underlinepublishing.com
USA

LUIZ BIRMAN

DEBIT CARD

The emotional side of money and credit

DEDICATION

Just as a structure must be built on strong pillars to be sustainable and long-lasting, I dedicate this work to the four essential pillars of my life.

To the memory of my father, Henrique Birman, my best friend, who taught me everything from the simplest concepts of finance to the deepest meaning of honesty.

To my dear mother, Fani, my unconditional supporter and guide.

To my beloved wife, Karla, my gift and partner in every moment.

And to my precious daughter, Bethânia, my greatest treasure, to whom I hope this knowledge will be useful throughout her life.

CONTENTS

PREFACE

This book was intentionally built as 26 chapters in a reflection plan about what money and resources represent, that constructive and destructive power. My suggestion is that you read one chapter each day of the month, starting on any day, and leave one day per week without reading, like a series that releases new episodes six days a week, so you build anticipation for the next lesson. At the end of four weeks, the reader will have completed a true reset in their financial and economic life and will carry the knowledge, read and applied, for the rest of their life.

I also suggest that this book become part of your personal "assets library," like that dream beach or mountain home you always want to visit again, so you keep valuing what you already have.

This work comes from a common misconception: that a debit card is limiting. Financial organization and being prepared for life, for the future, for balance, and for the unexpected is more than having credit or credit cards. It is learning to manage financial and economic resources,and above all, learning to handle money: what you earn, what you spend, and what you save.

Across the chapters, you will understand certain concepts, demystify others, and learn how to seek balance between what you want and what your life plans require focused on financial and emotional stability, which is so easily shaken and is at the root of many problems in the world.

CHAPTER 1

Money doesn't tolerate disrespect

There's a phrase that has been with me since long before I understood inflation, interest rates, or budgeting: ***"Money doesn't tolerate disrespect."***

I was a kid when I heard it for the first time, coming from a man who had already lived a lot—sitting in his armchair with black coffee in hand and the kind of look you get from someone who has lost a lot, yet is proud of having made it through life: my father.

He said it while looking straight into my eyes, as if he were handing me a treasure in the form of a lesson. That phrase has stayed with me as though it had been created for me, and now, from this point on, for you as well.

Back then I didn't fully understand what it meant, but I knew it mattered. Over time, that sentence became a guide. And today I can say it plainly: if you don't respect money, it disappears.

It doesn't matter how much you make. It can be one thousand or one hundred thousand. If you don't know how to handle money, it will slip through your fingers like water in a cracked cup. And do you know the biggest mistake of all? Thinking that because you earn well, everything is fine. That is the first act of disrespect.

Money is like people: it needs to be understood, taken care of, and, above all, respected. It has patterns. It has consequences. If you treat it like an enemy, it runs away. If you treat it like an ally, it grows. I'm not talking about mysticism here; I'm talking about practical behavior.

Because the way you treat money says a lot about the way you treat your own life.

In the end, money is a tool.

A tool to achieve security, comfort, freedom, and even generosity.

But for that to happen, you must put it in the right place.

Money is not identity.

Money is not love.

Money is not validation.

It is a resource. And like any resource, it must be managed.

I've met many smart, educated people with solid careers who are afraid to open their bank statements. And I've also met simple people with modest incomes who live in peace, with control in the palm of their hands. Do you know the difference between them? Awareness.

It's not about how much you earn.

It's about how well you understand what you earn, and what you do with it. Before we wrap up this first conversation, I want to leave you with a reflection I always carry:

> "Money doesn't change who you are."
> It only amplifies it."

If you're generous, you'll become more so.

If you're a consumerist, you'll spend more.

If you're mindful, you'll build more.

In other words: handling little well is training for when you have a lot.

So, respect every dollar. Every coin. It doesn't matter if you have little today. If you learn to treat what you have well, tomorrow you may have much more, along with the wisdom to use it.

And to close, here is your first challenge:

Today, still today, write down every expense you make. A coffee, a snack, a ride. Everything.

Start building awareness.

Tomorrow, do it again. And the day after, too.

You'll be surprised by what you discover.

Remember: ***"Money doesn't tolerate disrespect."***

That phrase is not just a saying.

It's a warning.

And it's also an invitation.

An invitation for you, starting now, to respect money the way it deserves, and to harvest the results in your life.

In the next chapters, we will talk about how to use a debit card intelligently, when and why to avoid credit, how to prepare to buy a home, build assets, create an emergency fund, and most importantly, how to do all of that without giving up your life, your dreams, and your peace.

This book is about freedom.

And freedom starts now.

CHAPTER 2

I only buy what I have money to pay for

Have you ever heard someone say: "Debit cards are for weak people. "Yes, I have, and I'm telling you without hesitation: that's one of the biggest financial myths out there. It's almost like saying, "It doesn't matter if I don't have money."

If there's anything that requires strength, it's looking at something you really want and telling yourself, "Not yet."

That is real strength.

Willpower. Awareness. Purpose.

I remember when credit became fashionable. Shiny plastic was status. Having a high limit was a sign of success. And the truth is that for a long time, many people believed that, including me, at first.

But the bill always comes. Always.

When you buy what you don't yet have the money to pay for, what you're doing in practice is borrowing against your future.

It's like saying: "I want this so badly today that I accept paying tomorrow—with interest, anxiety, and often guilt."

So, I'll ask you: is it worth it?

A debit card is not limitation. It is freedom.

Because when I use debit, I'm saying:

"I worked for this amount, it's in my account, and I'm choosing how to spend it."

It's a conscious purchase based on reality, not fantasy.

Here's a line I've carried for years:

"Debit is the card of truth."
Because it doesn't let you lie to yourself.

If the money isn't there, it says: **"No**."

That "no" hurts at first, but it becomes liberating over time.

Now tell me:

"How many times have you used credit not as a strategy, but on impulse?"

"How many times have you financed something that you could have waited a month or two to buy cash, with a discount, and without the weight?

You might say, "But Luiz, sometimes it's just a dinner, a shirt, a small payment."

I understand. No one is made of steel.

But repeated small mistakes are what create big problems.

It's the drip that wears down the stone, not the storm.

I often compare a misused credit card to that guest who shows up unannounced, stays too long, and then expects you to pay for dinner.

It enters harmlessly and even seems friendly. But when you notice, it has taken over your space, made a mess, and left debt behind.

Debit, on the other hand, is like an honest friend. It tells the truth. It reminds you of your limit. It teaches you to respect time.

Now, I'm not saying the credit card is the villain.

I use it myself, with awareness and strategy.

But never as a crutch.

Never as an escape to buy something my present cannot afford.

My debit card taught me something valuable:

"If I don't have it, I don't buy it." And if I want it, I plan for it."

That is the foundation of independence.

Independence is not having everything.

It is having the ability to wait.

To look at a desire and ask:

"Is this necessary right now?" Am I ready for this?"

If the answer is no, that's okay.

Waiting is wisdom.

Delaying is maturity.

Let me tell you a story.

I met a guy: let's call him "Gaston." He made good money and held a solid position at a reputable company. He was discreet, but he liked to live well: trips, brand-name clothes, a new car every couple of years. Everything financed.

Everything is on credit.

He always said: "I work hard, I deserve to enjoy life."

And he was right; he did deserve it.

But the problem was that he confused deserving with immediacy.

Life comes in seasons. And what you "deserve" today cannot cost what you will "need" tomorrow.

Gaston went broke.

Not because he didn't earn enough.

But because he spent based on what he "deserved," not on what he could actually afford.

And the saddest part? He didn't have real luxury. It was all an illusion of ownership—owned by stores, banks, and interest.

He kept paying for things he no longer evens had.

And he paid with stress, sleepless nights, and the feeling of always running to catch up.

That's not freedom.

That's modern slavery with a nice name.

So, when I say, "I only buy what I have money to pay for," it's not arrogance—it's wisdom built through mistakes.

"Have you ever been a "Gaston"? Taken steps bigger than your budget?' Then you already know how expensive that lesson can be.

But we learn. And I want you to learn without having to fall, no matter your age. It's never too early and never too late.

When you buy with what you have, you sleep in peace.

And that peace is priceless.

Knowing that everything around you is yours, paid for, settled, creates a feeling no credit limit can replace.

Buying with what you have also teaches you to value the process.

You plan, you wait, you organize, and then you buy.

That path builds financial character.

And financial character builds assets.

You know the saying, "Slow and steady wins the race."

It applies (strongly) to your relationship with money.

Every dollar you don't spend on impulse is a brick in the house of your security.

One day, that house will protect you.

Here's another line I carry as a personal philosophy:

"Paying cash is more than a financial decision. It's an act of self-respect."

Because when you pay with your own money, you're saying your freedom is worth more than immediate desire.

You give yourself a gift without giving yourself a debt.

That, my friend, is maturity.

We live in a world that pushes "now": the click, the instant delivery of everything.

But a solid financial life is built on the opposite: waiting, planning, and conscious choice.

So, I'll ask you:

"How many times did you buy something just to impress someone?"

"How many times did you spend filling a void that had nothing to do with the purchase?"

These questions aren't easy.

But they are necessary.

Because debit forces you to look inward before you look at the display.

It makes you think first.

That's the beauty of paying with debit. And notice: I'm not saying "debit card" every time, not by mistake, but by intimacy. When I say, "paying with debit," I mean I'm close to my finances. I know what I have, I know it's within my plan, and I can pay without creating problems later.

Credit gives you the false relief of "later."

And that "later" is almost always more expensive.

You don't need to become extreme.

But you do need to build awareness.

And awareness begins when you understand that every purchase is a decision about your future.

So, my invitation today is simple and powerful:

Spend one full day buying only with what you already have. No credit. No installments. No promises. Only what's in your account.
Write down how you feel.
Notice whether your sense of control grows.
Observe whether you start thinking twice before you pay.
This experience is worth more than any spreadsheet.
And remember:
"Those who live on what they have live in peace." Those who live on what they will earn live in debt to tomorrow."

CHAPTER 3

What is stability, anyway?

You know that word everyone chases, but almost no one can define it precisely? ***Stability.*** We hear it from early on: "Find a stable job." "You need stability in life."

"Buy a home: it's more stable."

But what is stability, anyway? And more importantly: who said stability looks the same for everyone?

For many people, stability means "not changing."

For a long time, people believed stability was finding a corner of the world, a fixed paycheck, health insurance, a paid-off car, and staying there.

Still. Safe. No risks.

But time, and life, show that stability is not the absence of movement.

It is the presence of balance.

You can be standing still and unstable.

You can earn well and still feel insecure.

You can own a home and still live afraid of losing everything.

Stability is not where you are.

It is how you are: with what you have.

Stable is the person who has breathing room.

Someone who can stop working for a while and still keep the bills paid. Someone who planned enough not to shake with every headline.

"Do you know the opposite of stability?"

It isn't chaos.

It's dependency.

Dependency on the next paycheck.

Dependency on credit cards, or other credit lines, to cover the basics.

Emotional dependency on impulse buying just to feel alive.

Here is the truth no one tells you:

Stability starts with awareness; not with a high salary.

I have met people bringing in forty thousand a month who lived anxious.

And I have met people earning four thousand who had peace, a plan, and the freedom to say "no" when necessary.

This is what I want you to understand from the start.

You don't have to wait until you're rich to have stability. You have to organize what you have and make the best of it.

Because stability is not stopping.

It is being able to choose to stop if you must.

To change if it's necessary.

To say: "I'm okay, because I prepared."

And that, my friend, can't be bought.

It is built.

Have you ever noticed how many people say they want stability, but when they get it, they feel bored, trapped, disconnected?

That happens because they confused stability with an empty routine.

Real stability gives you a base to move safely.

It's not an anchor.

It's a platform.

When you have stability, you can make mistakes without

collapsing. You can say "no" to a bad offer without fearing you won't cover the basics.

You can leave a toxic job because you have a plan.

You can postpone a purchase because you know peace is worth more than installments.

And do you know the secret to beginning building this?

Clarity about your real costs.

CHAPTER 4

Saving money isn't a punishment

For a long time, saving money was treated like a kind of punishment, as if it were a sentence handed down to people who couldn't afford to enjoy life.

If there's one line I've heard more times than I wish, it's this:

"I don't want to save money just to die later."

And I get it.

That sentence comes loaded with frustration, fear of deprivation, and stories from people who worked their whole lives, put money away, and still didn't get to live what they dreamed.

But I can tell you, with the conviction that life and numbers have taught me: saving money isn't punishment. Saving money is freedom.

Yes: freedom.

Saving doesn't mean giving up living. It means making sure you can live better, for longer, with more peace.

Because there is no real freedom when you depend on every dollar that comes in next month. There is no full rest when a single unexpected bill can knock you down.

And this is where we need to flip the switch:

Saving is taking care of yourself. Saving is saying "yes" to your future self.

It's saying: "I care about my future." I love myself enough to think about me one, five, ten years from now.

It's an act of self-care.

Just like you take care of your health, you should save money to take care of your security.

We need to learn how to deal with the famous fear of living ***"without."***

I understand when someone says saving money means depriving yourself—because culturally we were trained to think saving equals suffering.

But the real question is:

- "Enjoy what? For how long? And at what cost?"
- "Do you prefer five intense moments with fear of what comes next, or fifty consistent, calm moments with clarity and direction?"

Saving isn't an act of denial. It's an act of protection and projection.

The person who saves doesn't live less. They live with more awareness. Many people confuse saving with repression. But it's not about that. You don't need to stop grabbing coffee or cancel every simple pleasure. Saving is learning to say, "not yet" instead of "never again."

When you save, you trade immediacy for future freedom. And that freedom is worth far more than those shoes, that dinner, or that impulse purchase that feels good for one night and tightens your life for months.

"Want an example?"

Imagine you want to travel. You can put it on a credit card in 12 installments and spend a year paying for a trip that already ended—or you can save for a few months, go, and come back with the feeling that you earned it and that nothing is chasing you afterward.

Saving transforms consumption into achievement. And that changes everything.

The taste of something you pay for with effort and planning is completely different. It comes with peace, not guilt.

That's what saving is: freedom without shame.

Now, let's get to the point:

"Why do people resist saving so much?"

Because they were taught that "saved" money is money that's stuck. That it's useless. That it only matters when it's being spent.

And that's the big mistake: Saved money isn't stuck. It's being formed.

It's growing; even if slowly.

It's becoming calm, security, and opportunity.

And opportunity is what changes a life.

There are three truths you need to accept if you want to build financial freedom:

- **First**: no one can save for you.
- **Second**: you can't rely on the idea that "I'll figure it out later." Later is expensive.
- **Third:** saving is not about how much you earn. It's about how you organize what you earn.

People who earn a lot and don't save money are prisoners of their own lifestyle.

People who earn little and save something, anything, begin to build a way out.

And if you want a practical start, here's the most honest one:

Start small, but start now.

Save 1%. Save $10. Save what you can.

What matters is not the amount. What matters is the habit.

Because habit creates structure, and structure creates freedom.

You don't have to become cold or obsessive.

You just have to stop living like your future will magically take care of itself.

- **Saving is not punishment.**
- **Saving is love, with discipline.**
- **Saving is choosing peace over anxiety.**

And if you take one lesson from this chapter, let it be this:

When you have a reserve, you don't have to accept any job that appears. You can choose.

You can say no to the abusive client, the toxic boss, the contract that makes no sense.

And you can say yes to opportunities that only show up for people who are ready: a property priced below market, a promising partnership, a course that will accelerate your career.

The money saved is an invisible door-opener, and only those who prepared themselves can see those doors.

And here's what's most beautiful about it: saving isn't an act of restriction. It's an act of creation.

You're not cutting yourself down. You're shaping yoursel: preparing to be more, have more, and live better.

Saving is preparing yourself for the internal battle between the culture of "now" and the peace of "later."

We live in the era of "buy now, pay later," and that mindset is suffocating people.

We're surrounded by advertising, offers, and influencers telling us we must consume now, travel now, live now.

But no one talks about the bill that arrives. No one shows the anxiety of paying 12 installments for an experience that lasted three days.

No one teaches that saving is also living, just with dignity.

Saving is revolutionary.

In a world that wants you to spend everything you have, and what you don't havesaving is rebellion.

It's saying: "I don't need to prove anything to anyone. I am enough."

In the end, saving money gives you the one thing lack of control will never give you: choice.

The person who saves chooses what they want to live.
The person who saves chooses who they want to work with.
The person who saves chooses when to stop.
The person who saves chooses when to restart.
The person who saves chooses whether they continue or change everything.
And there's nothing more valuable than that.

Let me propose a shift in mindset: every time you think about saving, instead of thinking about what you're "losing," think about what you're gaining.

You're gaining quality time in the future.
You're gaining peaceful nights of sleep.
You're gaining the power to choose.
You're gaining emotional strength to deal with real life.

Saving money is like planting a tree. You don't harvest the next day. But one day (when the sun is strong and you're tired) there will be shade. And you'll be grateful you planted it.

Let me ask you a few questions for an honest self-check, so you can see the "power" of saving with different eyes:

Today, if you were fired, how long could you keep your life going with dignity?

"When was the last time you saved with intention, not by accident? What small luxuries could you reduce for three months to build your first reserve? What could you stop buying this month to save at least $50?"

If an emergency happened tomorrow, how much do you have set aside today?

Concerning, right?

Don't think big right now. Think real. Think practical. Think doable. And act.

Saving money isn't about punishment.

It's about respect. About love. About protection. About freedom. About vision.

And when you start to see it this way, saving stops feeling heavy and becomes one of the most satisfying habits in your routine.

CHAPTER 5

The cost of not planning

I want to start this chapter with a line of blunt wisdom: "If you don't plan, you pay twice: in money and in suffering."

"Have you noticed how, most of the time, the decisions that cost us the most were made on impulse?"

- That purchase without thinking.
- That "temporary" loan.
- That trip paid in installments that seemed harmless.
- That contract you didn't really read.
- That career decision made under pressure or fear.

All of that has a price, and I'm not talking only about dollars.

I'm talking about the emotional cost, the drained energy, the wasted time, the feeling of always chasing the damage you already did.

The truth is: a lack of planning is a silent debt.

You might not see it the day it's created, but over time it charges extremely high interest.

And the most dangerous part is that we get used to chaos.

We normalize improvisation.

We call it "real life" when, in reality, it's just the reflection of a lack of structure.

There's a myth that planning is for people who already have money. And that's one of the biggest financial mistakes you can make.

In fact, it's exactly the person who doesn't have much who needs to plan the most, because when you have little, every wasted dollar has impact. Every wrong step has consequences.

"So why do we avoid planning?"

Because planning requires stopping. It requires looking

at reality. It requires facing numbers, limits, choices, and consequences.

And most people were taught to avoid all of that.

We grew up under the doctrine of "let it happen," "we'll see," "I'll think about it later."

Meanwhile, life keeps moving. Problems grow. Dreams get postponed. Opportunities pass because we weren't ready.

Let's talk about real situations—the price of improvisation:

- A couple lives decently, but never sits down to organize finances together. Result: frequent fights, duplicated spending, conflicting decisions, and constant insecurity.
- A young person gets their first credit card without understanding how it works. They finance purchases, miss payments, get trapped in revolving credit—and now pay $1,200 for a $400 purchase.
- A micro-entrepreneur has a great idea, but never builds a spreadsheet, never projects costs, never separates business money from personal money. A few months later, the dream becomes debt, and the blame goes to "a bad market."

All of these cases share one thing: ***the absence of planning.***

"And do you know what scares me most?"

Many of these scenarios could have been avoided with two hours of attention and a notebook. But we weren't trained for that. We were trained to put out fires, not prevent them.

The false comfort of "next month will be better" is a classic:

- "This month was tight, but next month will be better."
- "It's just this card; next month I'll pay it off."
- "When I get my bonus, I'll get organized."

And what happens?

Next month is never better, because nothing changes if you don't change.

Money doesn't organize itself. Bills don't disappear because you have good intentions. Interest doesn't forgive anyone just because you're "trying."

As long as you live based on hope instead of a plan, you'll keep being a hostage to luck.

And luck is not a strategy.

Planning is.

Planning is freedom, not prison.

Another myth we need to drop is the idea that planning "kills spontaneity."

It's the opposite: people who plan have more freedom to be spontaneous.

- They can accept a last-minute invitation without guilt.
- They can buy a gift out of season without blowing the budget.
- They can say yes to an unexpected trip because they have a reserve.

Improvisation is only fun when you have structure. Without structure, it becomes desperation disguised as adventure.

And most importantly: people who plan to live with less fear.

And fear consumes more than any invoice.

"So how do you start planning without making it complicated?

I could give you complex tools, spreadsheets full of charts, apps, and indicators.

But I prefer to start with what actually works: the simple.

Step 1: Write down everything that comes in.
and everything that goes out in the month:
everything, even the bakery bread.
Step 2: Separate expenses by type: fixed, variable, discretionary, unexpected.
Step 3: Identify what can be adjusted, cut, or improved.
Step 4: Create realistic monthly goals
(save 5%, pay down a debt, make one conscious purchase).
Step 5: Review weekly and adjust as needed.

That's planning. It's clarity. It's seeing the road ahead.

It's not rigidity. It's awareness.

Planning isn't only to avoid disaster; it's mainly to build a future.

- Want to buy a home? Plan.
- Want to travel? Plan.
- Want to get out of debt? Plan.
- Want to have children? Plan.
- Want to change careers? Plan.
- Want to live better? Plan.

Whatever you don't plan becomes an emergency, and emergencies are always more expensive.

And if I can leave you with one piece of advice, it's this:

Plan ahead so you don't have to improvise in desperation.

- *"When was the last time you truly sat down to organize your financial life?"*
- *"What were your biggest losses because you didn't plan?"*
- *"And what can you plan this week that would save you headaches over the next few months?"*

Remember: the cost of not planning is too high.

It disguises itself as freedom, but it's a prison.

It arrives quietly, but when it hits, it can take everything down.

And the beauty of planning is that it doesn't demand perfection.

It only demands a decision: the decision to take care of yourself.

The decision to stop living on autopilot and start building with awareness.

Because in the end, it's not only about money. It's about life.

And your life deserves a plan: a plan that is yours, realistic, and powerful.

CHAPTER 6

Spending, cost, expense, and investment

In this chapter I want to teach you the fundamental differences between the four pillars of money in everyday life: spending, cost, expense, and investment.

We're going to demystify how these terms are used and show how these classifications completely change the way you think, spend, and plan.

Starting with Financial Awareness, let's get straight to the point: if you don't understand what to call what you're doing with your money, you'll live lost, and you'll pay dearly for it.

Why do some purchases hurt your wallet more than others?

Why do some people buy a lot and still prosper, while others keep "cutting back" and still sink deeper?

The answer is a single word: awareness. And it begins by understanding the nature of the money you move.

If I asked you right now: what would you classify as spending? And as an expense? What do you call a cost? And an investment?

If these words get mixed up for you, don't worry. A lot of people, even people who work with money , live in this confusion.

But from now on, we're going to put each thing in its place.

Because when you learn to name correctly what you do with your money, you gain power.

And as I always say: "If you don't know what you're doing with money, money is doing you."

Spending

Let's start with the famous Spending: what goes away without warning.

Spending is that movement of money that is often immediate, impulsive, or unnecessary.

It's the classic "just today."

It's "I bought it because it was on sale."

It's the daily snack that turned into a habit.

It's that impulse purchase, driven by emotion.

Spending is the kind of money that doesn't build anything lasting. It brings momentary pleasure, but almost always regret afterward.

Not that spending is wrong.

But you need to understand how much of your money is going away like this, and why.

Spending is when your money works against you.

Expense

Now let's go to Expense — what keeps you running.

Expense is different.

It represents the cost of your basic maintenance.

Electricity, water, internet, transportation, food, rent or a mortgage; all of that is expense.

They are the regular commitments that, one way or another, keep you alive and active.

But here's a crucial point: expenses also need to be monitored.

Because when they get out of control, you start living just to pay for the basics, and you stop growing.

Some people call everything a "fixed cost," but that's dangerous. Because when you say it's "fixed," you run the risk of believing it's untouchable.

And it isn't.

- You can change your cell phone plan.
- You can reduce your internet package.
- You can use public transportation more.
- You can review your grocery spending.

Expense is not destiny. It's a choice.

Even the fixed ones can be adjusted, if you want.

Cost

Cost, on the other hand, is what makes production possible.

Now we enter an area that many people confuse: cost.

Cost is everything that enables the generation of revenue.

It's more technical, more strategic.

If you have a business, costs are the inputs, the raw materials, what makes it possible to deliver your product or service.

But this also applies to personal life.

For example: the tuition for a course you need to grow in your career.

- Transportation to work.
- Your professional uniform.

All of that can be classified as cost.

Cost is closely tied to what generates return.

And that's why it must be evaluated with more criteria.

Cut costs without losing production, and you're evolving.

Cut the wrong cost, and you kill the engine that generates your income.

Investment

Finally, Investment: what makes you grow.

This is always the most loved, and at the same time, the most misunderstood.

A lot of people think investment is only buying stocks, a CD, or real estate.

But in reality, investment is anything you put money into today expecting a return tomorrow.

It can be financial, yes; but it can also be emotional, intellectual, strategic.

Investing is buying a book that changes your mindset.

It's paying for a consultation that reorganizes your life.

It's saving money to open your own business.

It's investing in a long-term fund so you can have a dignified retirement.

Investment is what expands your tomorrow.

Spending is what relieves your today.

And knowing the difference between the two is the beginning of freedom.

In this first contact, my goal was to show you that these four names — ***spending, expense, cost, and investment*** — are not just different words. They are different lenses through which you see your money.

And depending on the lenses you wear, you see a problem where there's a solution... and comfort where there's risk.

Money With a Name.

Now I want to introduce you to: Money With a Name.

If you want control over your money, the first thing you need to do is name what it is doing in your life.

Money without a name is money without a destination.

And money without a destination ends up in the wrong place.

Now that you understand the concept behind spending, expense, cost, and investment, let's move to practice.

Because it's no use knowing the theory if, when you're buying something at the grocery store, you still think "it's all bills" and that's it.

Let's imagine a common scene:

You went to the grocery store and bought:

- Rice, beans, and meat
- Beer and frozen French fries
- A premium chocolate
- A battery for the TV remote
- Laundry detergent and a new fabric softener that's more expensive than usual

In your head, maybe all of that falls into one category: groceries. But when you look closely, you realize that:

Rice, beans, and meat are basic expenses

Beer and French fries are nonessential spending

Premium chocolate can be emotional spending or an occasional treat, A battery is a functional replacement expense

More expensive detergent and softener can be spending disguised as an expense if they aren't necessary

Got it? The difference is in the intention and the impact.

If you swipe your card at the grocery store and think everything there is the same, you're missing the chance to understand how your money is behaving.

And, consequently, how YOU are behaving.

The role of awareness in organization is decisive!

Now let's go into a deeper analysis:

"What is the impact of classifying what you spend?"

Imagine two people with the same salary, the same rent, and the same basic cost of living.

One of them writes everything down and classifies their spending.

The other "keeps track in their head."

- *"Who do you think will have clarity at the end of the month?"*
- *"Who do you think will spot the waste?"*
- *"Who will know exactly what they can cut without compromising their life?"*

That's right: the one who gives it a name.

Because naming is organizing.

Organizing is understanding.

And understanding is acting with autonomy.

There's a question I often ask in the mentoring sessions I run: ***"Do you spend more out of necessity, emotion, or habit?"***

That answer changes everything.

- If you spend out of necessity, you need to adjust your budget.
- If you spend out of emotion, you need to look at what you're trying to fill.
- If you spend out of habit, you need to re-educate the way you operate.

And the key to discovering that is classification.

Write down everything you spend for one week. Everything.

Then look at it under a magnifying glass.

- "Is this an expense that keeps my life running?"

- "Is this spending that could be avoided or rethought?"
- "Is this a cost that generates future return for me?"
- "Was this an investment in me or in my future?"

This simple practice will change the way you see your $10, your $100, your $1,000, and your future resources (whether likely or not).

Reclassification Cycle.

Now I'm going to introduce what I call the Reclassification Cycle. Another important point is that the names change over time.

Something that is investment today can become a cost.

Something that looks like an expense can become spending.

And something that looked like spending can become an opportunity for re-education.

For example:

Your child's private school today is an important expense, but if it's taking too big a bite out of your income, it may be becoming unbalanced spending.

A health insurance plan may seem expensive now (an expense), but if it prevents a bigger expense later, it's almost a preventive investment.

The secret is to review periodically. Life changes. And the way you use money needs to change too.

Naming what we do with money is more than control.

It's respect for what you've achieved.

It's clarity to make better decisions.

It's the freedom to adjust before it's too late.

But I guarantee it isn't easy. As if the names changing throughout our lives weren't enough, there are also traps: confusing spending with investments — and how many people fall into a hole by fooling themselves with pretty words.

One of these classic examples is the lie of "***Personal Investment***."

We live in a time when everything has become an "investment."

You've probably heard phrases like:

- "Invest in yourself with this brand-new, top-of-the-line smartphone."

- "This car is an investment in your comfort and image."
- "This designer bag is an investment in your style and self-esteem."
- "This dinner is an investment in well-being."

And I ask you, completely honestly:

"Is that really an investment... or just pretty spending dressed up with a noble label?"

Not everything that's expensive is an investment. And not everything that feels good is worth the price you pay.

This is the kind of mindset that chains people to debt: emotional and financial.

Because when you label spending as investment, you silence your critical sense.

You allow yourself to go beyond what you can afford. You convince yourself you're doing something smart — when, in reality, you're rewarding yourself emotionally and going into debt rationally.

What defines a real investment is anything that will bring you a future return — in value, growth, stability, or income.

Something with a chance of multiplying or appreciating.

Something aligned with a strategic goal or purpose.

And something that can be measured in some way over time.

Now tell me:

- An $800 dinner at the trendy restaurant... does that fit?
- A $7,000 phone replaced for no real need... is that investment or digital vanity?
- An MBA you don't even want, just to please your boss... is that investment or submission?

If you're calling those things investments, you're not being honest with your reality.

And here's a big secret revealed:
marketing loves this confusion.
And there's more: this confusion is not a coincidence.
It's strategic.

Companies and brands have learned that if they call consumption "investment," you lower your guard.

You feel like you're evolving, when you're really just buying.

You see yourself as someone on an upward path, when you're only responding to ego impulses.

And that is dangerous!

Because every piece of spending disguised as investment has two losses: you spend more than you can, believing you're being smart, and you stop making the real investments that would actually bring you returns.

- "How many times have you seen someone drowning in debt but saying they "live well"?"
- "How many times have you seen people with an impeccable image, but a negative bank balance?"

That's not wealth. That's makeup.

True investment is quiet. Many times, it doesn't take pretty photos for social media.

- It's the amount you set aside every month, even if it's small.
- It's reading a book that expands your mindset.
- It's taking a class on Saturday morning while others are sleeping.
- It's a retirement plan that feels boring, but will preserve your dignity later.
- It's choosing to live somewhere simpler for a few years so you can save and build something bigger.

What doesn't show up in the feed is what builds your real freedom.

From today on, whenever you think about buying something and catch yourself saying:

"It's an investment."

Ask this question: "If it's an investment, what return do I expect?" In how long? And what real problem am I solving with this?"

If there isn't a clear, concrete, measurable answer...

Sorry. It's not an investment.

It's emotional spending. Period.

If you truly want to grow, you need to learn to look at what money builds, not at what it merely shows off.

The line between spending and investment is thin.

But it's that line that separates people who live for appearances from those who live with purpose.

Your Personal Classification System

Now I'm going to teach you how to build a simple personal system to categorize and review all your financial movements: at home, at work, or in your business.

You will learn how to apply this consistently, creating Your Personal Classification System.

Knowing what spending, cost, expense, and investment already give you a huge advantage over most people. But that only becomes useful if you turn that knowledge into action.

Financial intelligence without application is like a recipe with no food in the pot: it feeds no one.

So, I want to show you a simple, human, effective way to organize your entire financial life based on these four keywords.

And best of all: you can start today: no paid app, no complex spreadsheet, and no excuses.

- **Step 1 — Choose the tool you will actually use**

Before we talk about method, I need to remind you of something basic: The best tool is the one you can use frequently.

If you're a pen-and-paper person, you can use a simple notebook with four columns:

Spending | Expense | Cost | Investment.

If you prefer your phone, use a spreadsheet or even a notes app organized with emojis or hashtags (#investment, #expense).

If you already use apps, take advantage of the categories feature.

The important thing is not to overcomplicate it. Use what you will truly keep up with and review.

- **Step 2 — Record absolutely everything for 30 days**

This is the step that separates those who will change from those who are just excited.

For 30 days, record everything you paid and everything you received.

Down to the cents — the delivery order — even a simple $1 transfer or donation.

And every recorded item must be classified into one of the four columns:

- Spending — Was it emotional, impulsive, did it generate no return?
- Expense — Did it keep your life running?
- Cost — Did it help generate income or results?
- Investment — Will it give you a return in the future?
-

At first, it will feel like work. But it's like taking an X-ray of your choices. And nobody changes what they can't see clearly.

- **Step 3 — Review the data and find patterns**

After 30 days, stop and look at the whole picture.

You'll be surprised by what you find.

- "How much of your money has been spent on emotional spending?"
- "How much turned into expenses that could be optimized?"
- "How much did you really put into true investments?"
- "Was there any category that dominated your budget without you noticing?"

This analysis is pure gold.

It will show you where your leaks are, your unconscious repetitions, and your silent self-sabotage.

- **Step 4 — Set limits by category**

Based on what you observed, set realistic goals:

- "From now on, my emotional spending will not exceed 10% of my income."
- "I'm going to reduce variable expenses by 20%."
- "I'm going to increase my monthly investment by 5%."

That gives shape to your plan.

When you put numbers on what used to be just a feeling, control comes back into your hands.

- **Step 5 — Review weekly, adjust monthly**

You don't need to become a financial robot.

But you do need to create a minimal review routine.

Once a week — Sunday, for example.

Review what came in and what went out.

See whether the categories are balanced.

Once a month, adjust the limits. Observe your progress. Compare with the previous month.

This practice, done lightly and consistently, changes your life. "And the most beautiful part?"

- It doesn't depend on how much you earn, or your professional background, or how much financial math you know.
- It depends only on how much you want to understand and respect your money.
- It's not about spreadsheets. It's about awareness.

Some people make beautiful spreadsheets... and still have no control.

Some people have high income... and live in debt.

Some people read about finances... but never put anything into practice.

What will set you apart is the level of sincerity with which you look at yourself.

Organizing your money based on spending, cost, expense, and investment is an act of maturity.

It's saying: "Now I'm truly an adult — not only financially, but emotionally as well."

This new way of looking at money impacts your whole life — including your family decisions, your professional decisions, and your relationships.

Because the way you classify your money reveals, deep down, how you classify your values; by emotional depth, strategic impact, and connection to practical life.

Because the way we treat money is not only a technique; it's a direct reflection of who we are and what we believe.

Money Talks About You (And You Don't Even Notice)

If you stop and think calmly, the money that leaves your account every month is describing you as a person.

Your bank statements are not just numbers.

They are behavioral portraits.

They show:

- What you value
- What you repeat
- What you avoid
- What you ignore

And, most importantly, what you are building, or destroying, without realizing it

Money reveals more about your character than you imagine.

After all, who are you when it comes to money?

Are you the person who:

- Spends first and regrets later?
- Buys to feel valued or loved?
- "Consumes to compare yourself with others?"
- "Avoid looking at your bank balance because it hurts?"
- Or the one who plans, takes care of, and values every cent that comes in?

Each profile has an emotional root behind it.

And if you don't stop understanding how you deal with money, you will never be able to reorganize your financial life with awareness.

"What does your relationship with money say about your story?" Many people don't know this, but the way you use money today is directly tied to your emotional and family formation.

Maybe you come from a family where money was never talked about, so you repeat the silence; or money was always scarce, so you spend everything you have so you don't feel trapped; or money was used as control, so you rebel by spending compulsively.

Or money was worshiped, so you sacrifice yourself just to accumulate — but you don't live.

Understanding your past is essential to transform your present. Money doesn't change character. It reveals it.

There's a phrase I really like, and it applies perfectly here:

"Money doesn't change people."

It only reveals who they really are."

- If you're generous, you'll give more.
- If you're stingy, you'll hoard more.
- If you're unbalanced, you'll make mistakes more often and more intensely.
- If you're aware, you'll use money to build and to serve.

And all of that is embedded in how you classify your movements.

- "Do you spend on what you don't need?"
- "Do you invest in things you don't even believe in?"
- "Do you maintain expenses that drain you?"
- "Do you ignore costs that could become investments?"

The answer is between the lines of your transactions.

Money also affects your relationships

If there's one thing that causes wear and tear, crisis, and even separation in couples and families... it's the lack of clarity about how money is used.

- You want to grow, but your partner only spends.
- You want to invest, but your parents pressure you to consume.
- You want to save, but your friends mock your "stinginess."

What should you do?

Start by organizing your truth.

Show clearly what you are doing, why you are doing it, and what you are building with it.

Money communicates too. It can unite or divide.

But when you have awareness, you can inspire through example.

On the path of financial evolution, spending, cost, expense, and investment are not just financial categories: they are stages of maturity.

- When you spend too much, you're living on impulse.

- When you understand your expenses, you start organizing.
- When you identify costs, you start thinking like an owner.
- When you invest with purpose, you start building freedom.

Everyone who prospers consciously goes through these four stages.

The problem is most people stop at the second, and think they've done a lot.

But you're going beyond.

You're learning to think like someone who builds.

Like someone who doesn't just want money left over at the end of the month, but wants to make "money left over" a purpose in life.

So, before we move to the next chapter, I invite you to grab a bank statement from the last 15 days and classify each line as Spending, Expense, Cost, or Investment. Then answer:

- *"Which category dominated?"*
- *"Which one should be the biggest in your reality?"*
- *"Which one surprised you?"*
- *"Which one do you need to cut or balance?"*

Do it calmly, without judgment.

With the eyes of someone who is caring : not punishing.

The way you spend, maintain, produce, and invest your money is a mirror of the way you live.

If you want a more balanced, freer, and more meaningful life, start here.

This isn't about getting rich at any cost.

It's about using what you have with awareness, and what you're going to conquer.

CHAPTER 7

The weight of debt, and the value of relief

One of the best ways to learn about SPENDING, as we've already defined this "name" for money, is to reflect on how debt affects not only your wallet, but your emotional health, your relationships, and your view of the future.

I want to show you the Silent Noise of Debt, with its hidden, invisible, deep cost, and present a realistic path toward relief and regaining control.

- "Have you ever felt that weight nobody sees?"
- "That anguish that starts small, but grows with every phone notification?"
- "That cold sweat when you look at your bank statement?"
- "That feeling that your freedom has been confiscated by installments that seem to never end?"

That's debt.

It doesn't scream.

It whispers.

And those whispers become mental echoes that follow you all day long.

Debt has a destructive power that goes far beyond the number.

It steals your sleep, your focus, your mood, your self-esteem.

And if you've lived this , or you're living it, you know exactly what I mean.

Debt isn't only a financial problem. It's emotional.

A lot of people think the worst part of debt is the interest.

But the worst part of debt is the constant state of alert it installs inside you.

- You wake up thinking about money.
- You fall asleep asking yourself how you're going to pay.
- You avoid answering calls.
- You avoid checking email.
- You avoid going out with friends.
- You avoid opening the statement.
- You avoid talking with your family...

Debt doesn't isolate you only financially. It isolates you from life. And here's the point few people talk about:

- Long-term debt changes who you are.
- It makes you more reactive
- It takes away your patience
- It makes you insecure
- It keeps you from dreaming
- Debt traps your creativity.
- And creativity is exactly what you most need to get out of it.

When debt becomes identity, you start by saying: "I'm in debt." Over time, without noticing, you start thinking: "I am in debt."

Debt starts with the credit card, but it ends in your psychology.

And that transition is dangerous.

Because you stop fighting debt and start adapting to it.

You normalize it.

You accept it.

You settle into it.

You convince yourself you'll never get out.

And you stop trying.

So let me give you news that can change your life and your beliefs.

**"Debt is not a destiny.
It is a temporary condition that must be treated
with emotional urgency."**

But why do we get into debt?

Nobody wakes up and says: "Today I'm going to sink."

Debt slips in quietly, through the doors of carelessness, rush, or illusion.

Let's be honest: Sometimes you go into debt out of real necessity: a health issue, unemployment, or a family emergency.

Other times, out of lack of knowledge: buying without understanding interest, not comparing prices, and not planning.

And many times... out of vanity, impulse, or comparison.

It's painful to admit, but you can only get out of debt when you have the courage to look at its origin with truth.

The turning point begins with awareness before the solution

Before you think about renegotiating, selling assets, or earning extra income, you need to do something more important: recognize debt as an inflection point.

- It's showing you something.
- It's a signal.
- It's the symptom — not the cause.

And if you treat only the installment, but not the pattern that brought you there...

You may get rid of this debt, but you'll create another one later.Debt has to be defeated not only in your wallet, but mainly in your mind.

To overcome it and reach this level of awareness, you need to see the invisible impact of debt on relationships, mental health, and your view of the future.

Only then will you understand why getting out of debt is not just a financial goal: it's a process of personal rescue.

Debt lives between emotions. Nobody likes to talk about debt. But everyone has had it, has it now, or will have to face this topic at some point in life.

And when you don't talk about it, what happens?

Debt becomes even stronger.

It grows in silence.

It feeds on fear, shame, and procrastination.

What I'm going to tell you here is hard, but it's real: Debt doesn't destroy only your budget. It destroys your emotional life.

And it doesn't matter whether you earn a lot or a little — when you owe money, your world gets cloudy.

"Have you noticed how unresolved money issues are one of the main causes of breakups among couples and families?"

- It's not only about having or not having.
- It's the way people deal with money that separates them.
- One hides debt from the other.
- One spends, the other tries to hold the line.
- One wants to pay, the other prefers to look the other way.

Over time, what was "just a late bill" becomes a veiled criticism, a constant resentment, a disguised "I told you so," and eventually an emotional distance.

And before you know it, debt has become a third person in the relationship.

Always present, always tense, always between you.

Lack of financial clarity between couples creates distances bigger than miles.

Few people talk about this, but debt also makes the body sick.

Yes — the physical body. Insomnia, headaches, migraines, hair loss, anxiety, gastritis, binge eating, and so many others.

Many of these symptoms originate in chronic financial stress. And medicine already recognizes this:

When debt becomes a permanent state, your body interprets it as constant threat.

Your brain goes into "survival mode":

- It prioritizes the basics
- It blocks complex decisions
- It reduces your ability to concentrate
- It increases your irritability

- It drains your vital energy

In other words, you're not "tired of life." You're tired of not seeing a way out.

There's one more thing few people notice: debt limits your dreams without you realizing it.

"How many times have you skipped a course because you thought it was too expensive?"

Given up on a trip?

Turned down an invitation because you feared the bill?

Decided not to buy a gift for someone special?

Or simply stopped dreaming because you believe "it's not possible anymore"?

This is what I call the invisible prison of debt.

It doesn't lock you up with bars.

It locks you up with ideas, like:

- "I'll never be able to."
- "It's not for me."
- "I'm past that stage."
- "Maybe next year."

But debt should not define your story.

It's a phase , and like every phase, it can be overcome with direction, courage, and clarity.

Debt has a solution, but not magic , and that's why I decided to write this book.

Many people look for a shortcut.

A loan to pay another loan

A new credit card to cover the old one

A high-risk bet in the hope of winning fast

But I'm telling you firmly: debt is solved with reality, not with magic. You need to lay everything out. See the total. Organize. Negotiate truthfully.

Stop dodging calls.

Build a realistic strategy.

And most importantly: change the behavior that created this debt. Because paying without changing is repeating.

And repeating is the shortest road to sinking again.

So, let's organize the chaos!

Let's understand the different types of debt, how to evaluate them, what to prioritize, and where to start with clarity, practical structure, and accessible language.

Let's create a turning point (a concrete action) for those who want to get out of suffocation.

For that, I'm going to share something simple and precious I learned throughout my life in the financial market:

**Not all debt is the same,
and not all debt should be treated the same way.**

There are debts that are like a small scratch: they bother you, but they heal quickly.

And there are debts that are like deep wounds: if not treated urgently, they can paralyze you.

A big mistake many people make is treating everything the same. Or worse: treating nothing, because the whole thing feels too big. The secret is to separate before you add.

When bills start piling up, the first emotional reaction is to generalize.

- *"I owe a lot."*
- *"There's no solution."*
- *"It's over — I'm screwed."*

But when you open everything calmly and separate it, you realize not everything is as urgent as it looks. And some cases have a simple and quick solution, if they're handled with focus.

Four main types

I classify debts into four main types: all of which deserve attention:

- **1. Urgent and essential debt**

Example: past-due rent, electricity about to be shut off, children's school, food.

These need to be handled immediately, because they threaten your basic stability.

Here, there is no emotional negotiation.

You need to act: renegotiate, cut nonessentials, and prioritize these payments until you stabilize.

- **2. High-interest debt that grows fast**

Example: credit card revolving balance, overdraft, loans with abusive interest.

These are the ones that silently kill you.

Even if the amount seems small, the growth is accelerated.

Here, the rule is: stop the growth as fast as possible.

Two main options:

- Replace it with a lower-interest debt, for example: secured credit or payroll-deducted loans tied to recurring payments such as salary or retirement, refinancing with different institutions , perhaps government-backed where incentives are higher and interest is lower, and other options along the same lines.
- Renegotiating directly with the creditor to get a fixed, clear installment plan is also always a great path , but watch the rules and the upfront costs of any change.

Remember: negotiate. NEVER accept anything at any price!

Likewise, never ignore the credit card revolving balance. It's like a gasoline leak, invisible, but highly explosive.

3. Emotional and disguised debt

Example: buying a new phone on installments without needing it, financing a car for status, paying for a course you don't use just to say you "do something."

These debts are more subtle.

They don't seem urgent, but they reveal mental and emotional patterns.

Many times, they are funded by comparison or vanity.

What should you do?

- Recognize the motivation
- Interrupt the pattern (don't renew it, don't repeat it)
- Pay it, but use the learning as a vaccine

These debts teach much more about you than about interest.

- **4. Structured and planned debt**

Example: a mortgage with a negotiated rate, student loans with low interest, consortia plans.

These are not exactly "good," but they can be strategic.

As long as they fit in your budget, with a realistic payoff forecast, they don't suffocate you; they organize you.

Here's the tip:

- Keep payments current.
- Review the rate and term annually.
- Make sure they don't exceed 25% to at most 30% of your income

But remember: taking on this type of debt requires planning.

Because if, to keep payments current, you use an overdraft or a credit line, you're increasing the final cost of the debt exponentially, and the end result can be disastrous!

"So how do you prioritize what to pay or handle first?"

Now that you understand the nature of debts, you need to organize your order of attack.

Keep your basic structure alive: water, electricity, housing, food, and health.

Cut the high interest before it grows: credit cards, overdraft, personal credit.

Negotiate whatever can be renegotiated.

Own the emotional mistakes with humility and a commitment to change.

Keep structured debts under control — but without panic.

Debt doesn't disappear by being ignored. It disappears by being faced. If there's one thing I learned in practice, it's this: "The more you pretend debt doesn't exist, the more it grows in silence."

And do you know what grows along with it?

Guilt.

Shame.

Self-sabotage.

But when you say:

"Okay. This is it. I owe. And I'm going to fix it."

Everything starts to change.

You stop being a hostage and become the driver of your own solution. Getting out of debt is a process that begins with a practical plan, adapted to the reality of where you live and accessible even for those in a delicate situation with little money.

Here you start regaining real control, learning to prioritize, cut, communicate, negotiate, and above all, recover your power of choice.

War Plan — Getting Out of Debt Strategically in 7 Steps

I call this the *War Plan — Getting Out of Debt Strategically in 7 Steps*. Up to this point, we talked about awareness, emotion, types of debt, impacts, and common mistakes.

Now it's time for action. The turning point has arrived.

Because debt is not solved with motivation alone.

It's solved with a plan. Clarity. Order. Decision. Persistence.

And so your liberation from debt becomes real (your personal success case) I'm going to give you the exact step-by-step I developed and have guided hundreds of people through, including business owners with large debts and also people earning minimum wage.

Yes, it worked for many, and it will work for you too.

Because it doesn't matter how much you owe. What matters is how you deal with what you own.

This is where your financial emancipation plan begins:

- **Step 1 — List all debts. Yes, ALL of them.**

You need to see the real size of the situation.

Paper, spreadsheet, or phone in hand.

First write down who the creditors are: banks, credit cards, companies, financing, pharmacy accounts, grocery accounts, or other informal ones (the ones without documents or a contract but that are part of your day-to-day).

And no less important: individuals , especially when they are close, like friends and family, because they can be the ones that shake you emotionally the most, whether because of the creditor's pressure or your own internal pressure.

Now find the total amount and the installment amounts.

Identify, calculate, and find the monthly or total interest, even if approximately, and don't be ashamed to ask for technical help if you need it.

Seeking a solution is a reason for pride, not shame!

Next, define the current status of each debt: separate into current, past due, renegotiated, or ignored.

Separate by debt type, as we learned earlier: essential, high-interest, emotional, and structured.

Remember: you can't fight an enemy you can't see. Naming is the first act of regaining control.

- **Step 2 — Rank by urgency and impact.**

Now that you have a clear view, classify them into three levels:

- Critical: risk of service shutoff, eviction, negative credit report, risk of lawsuit, or severe emotional impact.
- Important: growing interest, with an urgent need to renegotiate.
- Manageable : under control or that can wait.

ALWAYS start the attack with what can destroy your stability.

Then attack high interest.

Only then deal with the rest.

- **Step 3 — Review your current financial reality**

Before you promise payment to any creditor, you need to know:

- Exactly how much comes in each month;
- How much goes out in fixed and variable expenses;
- How much is left over (or how much is missing).

This is called a real action base.

You need to know your "room to maneuver," even if it's zero today. Because even with negative room it's possible to create a solution, but only with truth.

- **Step 4 — Cut, reallocate, and negotiate.**

Here comes the real adjustment plan:

- Temporarily cut nonessential spending: streaming subscriptions, delivery, and anything that may be nice but can come back when things are more balanced. And I guarantee it will be much more appreciated then.
- Renegotiating directly with creditors: many prefer to receive less than to receive nothing.
- Consolidate debts if possible (swap high interest for lower interest).
- Use extra inflows like a year-end bonus, a bonus check, selling items, or even assets to solve the problem , not to spend.

Attention: any extra income without a clear purpose becomes invisible spending.

- **Step 5 — Communicate and involve those who live with you**

If you live with other people, you need to be transparent.

- Show the reality.
- Share responsibility , without blame.
- Ask for help, support, and patience.
- Explain that this is a rebuilding phase and that the sacrifice is temporary.
- Hidden debt becomes double trouble.

When everyone knows, it's easier to prioritize and cooperate.

- **Step 6 — Set real, celebrate-able goals**

You need to win. Even small ones.

- Pay the first past-due bill and celebrate.
- Negotiate and reduce interest, and recognize your attitude.
- Get out of negative credit status and mark the milestone.
- Get to the end of the month without paying bills late, and congratulate yourself.

Your emotions need positive fuel to stay in the game.

Wins reinforce your brain that you are in control : which helps you gain clarity and make better decisions.

- **Step 7 — Create a behavior commitment**

There's no point paying the debt and repeating the pattern.

So commit to:

- Not buying on installments without planning;
- Not taking on new debt while paying old debt < or taking on more aggressive debt , until everything is paid off;
- Not falling into comparisons with others; and

Learning to plan before you consume.

If you want, write it down. Sign it. Keep it in your wallet or stick it on the refrigerator door.

Turn your decision into an alliance with yourself.

I want to tell you something now that maybe nobody has ever told you this directly, in plain words:

- You are not your debt!
- You may be in debt, yes.

But that does not define who you are.

Nor what you're worth.

Nor what you can build starting today.

Debt is just a financial trail. Your identity is much bigger than that. When you zero out a debt, even a small one, something powerful happens: you regain the right to dream.

It may sound poetic, but it's real.

You start breathing better, sleeping more peacefully, thinking clearly, making plans again, and regaining self-esteem.

That has no price.

It's like taking a weight off your chest.

It's like opening a window after being locked in a dark room for a long time.

Debt leaves marks. But it also leaves lessons. And those lessons can become the pillars of your new financial life.

- You learn to be more selective.
- You discover you can live with less.

- You understand the true value of things.
- You start consuming with purpose, not with guilt or emptiness.
- You learn to say no, including to yourself.

Getting out of debt is not only getting out of the red.

It's entering a new lifestyle.

Knowing, or rediscovering, the symbolic and emotional value of being "debt-free," and keeping control after you get out of the hole, is about freedom.

It's about rebuilding; responsibility; and a vision of the future. Relief isn't at the end: it's at the restart.

Sometimes we may fall again, but if that happens with awareness, and with these teachings we shared, the path to a solution will be lighter and shorter. In fact, at times you may even need to resort to some kind of credit. But now, with the understanding you're gaining here, your posture will be different.

This debt will be planned debt.

For that, you must ask before acting:

"Is this essential?"

- "Does it have abusive interest?"
- "What is my plan to pay for it?"
- "What am I trying to solve with this purchase?"
- "What used to be impulse will now be choice."
- "What used to be emotional will now be strategic."

A life without debt is not a life without effort. It's a life with clarity.

You will still have bills.

You will still make difficult choices.

You will have to say no, cut here, adjust there.

But you will do all of that with awareness. With autonomy. With direction.

Because the worst debt is not with the bank: it's with your peace of mind.

When you get rid of external debt, you can finally pay off internal debt and live at peace with yourself.

But remember: debts taken to build assets can be considered investments if they are managed correctly and created with planning!

Now I want to suggest you take 10 minutes and write two very short lists:

"What has debt taken from me so far?"
"What will financial freedom a
llow me to do from now on?"

If you want, stick these lists on the bathroom mirror, on the cover of your notebook.

Review them every week.

Because the greatest fuel for someone who wants to get out of debt is remembering what's at stake.

You made it this far.

You read everything. You reflected. You looked inward.

And most importantly: you owned your desire to change.

Now you have not only the tools, but also the vision and the emotional strength to turn this around.

In the next chapter, I'll teach you what portion of what you earn can be SPENT.

Because understanding how to avoid debt starts with understanding how much, and how, to spend.

CHAPTER 8

How much of what I earn should I spend?

Have you ever asked yourself this: really asked it? *"How much of what I earn can I actually spend?"*

It's not how much you WANT to spend.

It's not how much the bank ALLOWS you to spend.

It's how much you SHOULD spend to live a balanced, calm, sustainable life.

That question is a master key. When you answer it honestly, you start making decisions based on reality, not emotion.

You begin to break the illusion of "I'll figure it out later."

Want to know the most common mistake? People live as if their entire paycheck is available.

You earn $5,000? You spend $5,000.

Or worse: you spend $6,000 on the card, believing that "next month it'll even out."

That's an illusion. It's like driving without brakes. It works... until the first pothole.

Your paycheck (your monthly incom) needs a destination before it hits your account. That is one of the biggest truths I can teach you. Your money needs a plan before it arrives. If you wait for it to land and then decide, you've already lost the match.

Money without purpose becomes consumption without criteria. And the result is the same old story: too many installments, out-of-control statements, no emergency fund, and that false feeling of "I make good money, but I never see it."

The three-bucket method

Let's talk about proportion: the three-bucket method.

To make your life easier, I'm going to give you a simple, direct, highly practical model. It's a smart adaptation of the 50/30/20 approach, adjusted to real lif, even across different countries and realities.

Think of your monthly income as three buckets:

- **Bucket 1 — Essentials (50%)**

Everything that keeps your basic life running:

- Housing (rent or mortgage payment)
- Food
- Transportation
- Utilities (water, electricity), internet
- Basic healthcare
- Education (when applicable; and yes, education is a great investment—when planned)

This bucket should consume at most 50% of your take-home income.

If it's taking 60%, 70% or more, that's a warning sign. You're living above your baseline structure. Adjustments are needed—urgently, if possible.

- **Bucket 2 — Quality of Life (30%)**

This bucket is for living—enjoying life with intention:

- Leisure and entertainment
- Personal purchases
- Subscriptions and non-essential services
- Gifts
- Personal care
- Small wants and treats

This bucket matters. Don't live like a monk waiting for a day you'll finally "be rich." You need quality of life along the way. But be careful: pleasure without planning becomes emotional debt.

- **Bucket 3 — Building Your Future (20%)**

This is where the "magic" happens:

- Emergency fund

- Investments
- Savings for goals
- Debt repayment (if applicable)

This is the bucket that creates freedom. It makes sure tomorrow won't be a painful repeat of today. This is where you plant the seeds of peace.

"But my month already starts in the red!"

I know. Many people read this with the reality that they spend more than they earn.

But the goal here isn't perfection. It's progression.

If today 100% goes to essentials, your first step is to reduce that to 90%. Then 80%. Then 70%, until you reach the ideal percentage (or as close as possible, as fast as you can).

The secret is the trend, not rigidity. Even with little, you can start building a healthier split. Adapt the method to your reality, without guilt.

"This doesn't work for me. I can barely pay rent."

And you may be right: the "pure" model won't fit everyone right away. But it serves as a referenceyour north star, your direction.

Over time, you adjust your path so that direction fits your life."What if your income is tight or variable?"

If you're self-employed, earn commissions, have good and bad months, or live on a very small paycheck, you know you can't run a rigid month-to-month script.

But you can build a decision baseline. The key is to separate "great months" from "normal months," and never spend in a weak month what only works in a strong one.

Try this:

- Pick a conservative "reference income" to plan with (for example: plan on $2,000 even if good months bring $2,500).
- Spend based on the reference number, not the best case number.
- Save the surplus from stronger months to cover weaker months.

This is a conservative reference-budget approach. It saves people from the emotional-financial roller coaster.

It also resembles how many high-quality-of-life households plan: looking at the year as a cycle, not just one month at a time.

Two practical examples (with approximate numbers):

- **Case 1: João, fixed income of $1,800.**

João lives alone, pays rent, spends a lot on transportation, and still has an outstanding loan. His budget is basically fully consumed: about $1,000 on housing and fixed bills, roughly $500 on food and transportation, and around $300 on card/loan payments. Total: $1,800, nothing left.

Adjustment plan:

- Renegotiate the loan to reduce the payment.
- Share housing or move to a place with lower rent.
- Cut back on delivery and restaurants; cook more, or buy portioned meals (often cheaper and healthier).
- Start a micro-reserve: $10 per week. Yes, $40/month is a beginning.

Goal: gradually free up 5% for reserves and 5% for small pleasures.

- **Case 2: Ana and Marcos, couple with combined income of $5,000.**

They have a young daughter, pay school, rent, and two phone financings. They feel they "only spend on necessities," but they can't save.

Current split (approx.): about $2,200 in rent and bills; around $1,200 for food and school; roughly $800 in financings; and about $800 in leisure, delivery, clothes, and "little purchases."

Adjustment plan:

- Pay off the phones faster and stop financing everything.
- Rebuild monthly shopping with a list and fewer impulse trips.
- Replace restaurant weekends with at-home or free activities.
- Create a physical or digital "monthly reserve envelope," starting with $100.

Without changing jobs, this couple can move from 0% saved to 10% saved with lighter, smarter adjustments.

The most important thing is consistency. It's not about saving a lot. It's about saving always, even if it's $20/month. The gesture creates a habit, and habits change everything.

A consistent saver beats an occasional saver.

You don't need to be a spreadsheet expert to start.

Use whatever is simplest: a personal finance app, writing everything down for 30 days (yes, with a pen), physical or digital envelopes for the buckets, weekly reminders on your phone; what matters is looking at your money before it leaves.

The most dangerous saboteur: you, and the invisible leaks in your budget. You make the plan. You set the goals. You organize the spreadsheet. You divide the buckets. But then... the month happens.

And when you look again, the money has evaporated.

That's what I call an "invisible leak": small, frequent, disguised decisions that, added together, destroy your plan.

- **Error 1: The self-deception of "just this once."**

"Just this month." "Just this little shirt." "Just this dinner." "Just this installment."

"Just this once" is self-sabotage's most convincing argument, because it looks harmless. But it repeats... and repeats...

An extra $30 per week equals $1,560 per year, and you barely notice it.

- **Error 2: Financing without a plan.**

Installments became the default in many places: 10 payments, 12 payments, 24 payments.

Then your card becomes a cemetery of past purchases. You pay for what you don't even use anymore, and worse, you spend income you haven't earned yet.

Financing without planning is spending the future in the present with the weight of the past.

Practical rule: only finance if
(1) it's necessary,
(2) the payment fits your budget even by itself,
and
(3) your total monthly installments do not exceed about 30% of your income.
Otherwise: think twice.

- **Error 3: Looking at the payment and ignoring the total.**

"This payment is only $70..." , but when you add everything up:

- $70 for the TV
- $180 for the phone
- $250 for dental work (note: medical necessity is different from cosmetic extras)
- $40 for a subscription
- $90 for a "course" you don't really need
- $120 for last month's card balance

Total: $750. And you thought everything was under control.

Always look at the monthly total. The weight is in the set, not the pieces.

- **Error 4: Spending as if you've already received the money.**

This is the "mental advance", spending on the assumption that a bonus will come, a tax refund will arrive, a contract will close.

And if it doesn't, you fall into improvisation.

Rule: only treat money as real when it's already in your account. Remember: this is a DEBIT mindset. Dreams are dreams. Planning requires reality.

- **Error 5: Confusing "I deserve it" with "I can afford it."**

This one is emotionally tricky because it starts from something real: the desire for reward.

You work hard. You sacrifice. Then the impulse comes: "I deserve it," and you buy.

The problem is when "deserve" becomes a license to lose control.

You do deserve good things, but you also deserve to sleep peacefully, without fear of next month's bills.

Practical rule: set a monthly self-reward amount inside Bucket 2. Use it with joy, and with awareness. Don't exceed it with emotional excuses.

Your mind also sabotages you. The brain hates saying "no," so it creates clever rationalizations:

- "It's on sale."
- "Prices will go up later."
- "I'm investing in myself."
- "It's just today."
- "I'll figure it out."

Recognizing the pattern is half the cure. Unplanned spending disguises itself as "need," but it's just impulse with an argument.

Correcting your course and restarting matters more than getting it perfect.

There comes a moment when it hits you. You look at your bank statement, feel that cold knot in your stomach, and think: "I lost control." Or worse: "It's over; there's no solution."

Here's a liberating truth: it's never too late to restart.

The difference between people who prosper and people who drown isn't the mistake: it's the decision to correct.

First step: stop punishing yourself. Guilt doesn't pay bills. It builds nothing. Replace guilt with awareness and action.

You can't change the past, but you can prevent it from repeating on the next statement.

"Gold sequence"

The "gold sequence": restructure your buckets after the chaos.

- **Step 1 — Look with honesty.**

Write down everything you spend today: no censorship, no self-deception.

Check which bucket (essentials, pleasure, future) is being ignored or exaggerated.

- **Step 2 — Redefine possible targets.**

If today 70% goes to essentials, that's okay. Start by aiming for something like:

• 20% quality of life
• 10% future

Then move toward:

• 60% essentials
• 25% pleasure
• 15% future

And so on. The point is the trend toward balance.

- **Step 3 — Commit to one adjustment per month.**

Don't try to fix everything at once; that only creates frustration. Choose one target at a time:

- Cut $100 in unnecessary spending.
- Reduce delivery by one order per week.
- Save $50 per month, without fail.
- Pay one debt down before buying something new.

Small adjustments change trajectories. It's the domino effect, working in your favor.

"What can you cut without harming your life?"

When you review your budget, ask yourself:

- *"Is this essential, or just a habit?"*
- *"Does this move me toward my goal—or away from it?"*
- *"If I cut it, will it truly hurt me emotionally—or just my ego?"*

You don't need to cut the coffee with a friend if it feeds your soul. But you may need to cancel the subscription you never use, or the "ghost gym." The right cut is the one that frees you without wounding you.

Rebuilding takes patience—but it pays off. Over time you realize you don't need everything you thought you needed. The peace of control is worth more than the pleasure of an impulsive purchase.

You don't need to be radical. You need to be consistent. Don't compare your 3% with someone else's 30%. Start where you are—but do it every month.

Money likes people who care for it frequently, not perfectly.

The Real Split Exercise

Now it's time to build your real plan: splitting your income with purpose.

No magic formulas. No rigid rules. No guilt. Just realism, clarity, and commitment.

You're not competing with anyone. You don't need to get it all right today. Your plan will evolve with you.

- Stop for 15 minutes and look at your income with new eyes.
- How much you earn doesn't define your success.
- How you distribute what you earn defines your freedom.

I call this: The Real Split Exercise.

- **Step 1 — How much do you earn?**

What is your average monthly take-home income? Do you have additional sources (side jobs, rent, commissions)? Is your income fixed or variable? Use a conservative average as your base.

- **Step 2 — How much do you spend today?**

List approximate monthly amounts for:

- Housing
- Transportation
- Food
- Fixed bills
- Credit card
- Installments
- Healthcare
- Leisure
- Personal purchases
- Investments
- Donations or help you provide
- Other outflows

Now total it up and compare with your income. Did you save, break even, or overspend?

- **Step 3 — How are your buckets today?**

Estimate the percentage going to (1) essentials, (2) quality of life, and (3) future (investments, debt, reserves). If any bucket is below 10%, pay attention. If the future bucket is at 0%, that's a red alert.

- **Step 4 — Your 90-day target split.**

Write an ideal split for the next 90 days—nothing extreme, but real. For example:

- 60% essentials / 25% quality / 15% future
- 70% essentials / 20% quality / 10% future

That becomes your GPS, even if you're still far from it today.

- **Step 5 — The commitment.**

Answer honestly:

- "What can I adjust this week to move toward that split?"
- "What expense can I cut without pain?"
- "What behavior can I change with awareness?"

If you want, write it down, sign it, and place it somewhere visible. A plan without commitment is just a pretty idea. A plan with action becomes a new future.

One certainty: nobody will take care of your money for you, not the bank, not the government, not your employer. You will.

And the sooner you know what you can spend, the sooner you'll have the freedom to spend with peace.

Spending consciously is more enjoyable than spending on impulse, because it brings peace. And peace is worth more than any possession.

CHAPTER 9

Kids can learn finance too

This chapter might be my favorite. On its own, it could become a whole book.

Think of it like planting a seed for a strong tree: your family's financial culture. Strong roots, healthy reserves, the ability to cross every season, blooming, bearing fruit, renewing when needed. As I always say: the piggy bank should be the first school.

Let me start with a question: when was the first time you heard the word money?

Maybe someone handed you a few coins and said, "Put it in your piggy bank." Maybe you heard an adult complain, "We don't have money for that." Or maybe you grew up in a house where money was never discussed.

The truth is: our relationship with money doesn't begin in adulthood. It begins in childhood; quietly, but deeply.

Childhood shapes financial thinking even when no one "teaches finance." Not teaching is still teaching, just in a destructive way.

It's like leaving fertile land uncultivated. Weeds grow on their own. And what grows? Fear. Greed. Impulsiveness. Guilt. Lack of control.

So, let's make one rule clear, almost a mantra:

Kids can, and should, learn about money. And the good news: it doesn't require boring classes or advanced math. It requires experience, conversation, and example.

The piggy bank is the first MBA.

The classic piggy bank, pig, can, jar, or even an app, may still be the best financial laboratory for a child.

This simple object and habit teach four big lessons:

- Money has value.
- Saving today enables tomorrow.
- Choosing is part of the proces: you can't have everything.
- Waiting pays off.

When a child saves for something they want, they often learn more about money than many adults holding a credit card.

Different ages need different approaches. Financial education doesn't have to be rigid. Here are simple ideas by age:

- **Ages 3–5**
- Show coins and explain that each one has "power" (it can buy something).
- Play buying and selling with toys.
- Encourage saving a few coins in the piggy bank.

- **Ages 6–9**
- Introduce the idea of a small allowance (weekly works well).
- Split money into three small jars: spend, save, give.
- Help set simple goals ("I'll buy a toy in two months").

- **Ages 10–13**
- Involve them in small household decisions (e.g., comparing prices at the grocery store).
- Show where money comes from (salary, work, effort).
- Talk openly about wins and mistakes with money.
- Keep the language light, natural, part of daily life. It doesn't require spreadsheets. It requires presence.

"But what if I never learned this the right way?"
That's one of the questions I hear most.
"How can I teach what I don't know?"

My answer is simple: you don't have to know everything. You have to care.

Learning together is an act of love and humility.

Why not start saving together? Or planning a family purchase? Or creating a challenge: "Who can save the most this week?"

Your child, nephew, godchild, student, doesn't need a perfect teacher. They need an example.

Money is not a taboo: it's a tool.

For years, many people treated money talk with kids as:

"Not a children's topic." "A rich people thing." "An adult concern." "A subject that causes conflict."

But what really happens when we don't talk?

Kids grow up without references. They learn from ads, social media, and friends, often with no foundation.

They form limiting beliefs: "Money is bad." "Rich people are greedy." "Poor people have no choice."

Silence also educates, and usually, it educates the wrong way.

The three-coin method: spend, save, give.

If I could teach every child only one money lesson, it would be this: money has three destinations—and you must learn to choose.

It's simple. And it's transformational.

Spend. Save. Give.

This trio is more than a way to split coins. It's character formation.

Through it, a child learns to handle immediate pleasure (spend), develop self-control and long-term vision (save), and cultivate empathy and social awareness (give).

- **Coin 1 — Spend (with choice and responsibility)**

Teaching spending may sound strange, but it's essential. Conscious spending is one of the most important adult skills.

The ideal time to learn is when mistakes are still cheap. Better a child spends $10 poorly and learns, than an adult spends $10,000 poorly and calls it normal.

How to apply:

- Give a symbolic amount and let them choose what to buy.
- Talk before: "What do you want? Is it worth it? How long will you use it?"
- After the purchase, ask: "Are you happy with your choice?"

If they regret it, great. Regret teaches more than prohibition.

The goal isn't a perfect purchase. It's thinking before, choosing with intention, and learning from the result.

- **Coin 2 — Save (with purpose and patience)**

Saving is the first step toward freedom. But saving with no goal is hard, even for adults.

So, the lesson isn't "save just to save." It's: save to achieve something you want more than the impulse of right now.

How to apply:

- Help the child choose a goal (a toy, a trip, a special gift).
- Calculate together how much to save per week/month.
- Create a separate jar/envelope just for that goal.
- Make progress visible ("Look—we're already halfway there!").

This teaches that saving isn't suffering. It's postponing with purpose. and time can be an ally, not an enemy.

- **Coin 3 — Give (with empathy and awareness)**

This is the most powerful lesson, because it goes beyond money: it's character.

Giving teaches that money isn't only for me, that there's always someone with less, that I can be part of the solution, and that happiness can come from generosity.

Giving doesn't shrink you. It expands your perspective and your sense of meaning.

How to apply:

- Let the child choose a portion to help someone.
- It can be simple: food, a toy, clothes, a small contribution.
- If possible, deliver together, or share stories of impact.

- Reinforce: it's not an obligation. It's a privilege to be able to choose to help.

Practical tip: the three jars (or envelopes)

Create three containers—physical or digital:
- Jar 1 — "Now" (spend when you want)
- Jar 2 — "Later" (save for something bigger)
- Jar 3 — "Share" (help someone or a cause)

Do it together, and show that you also split your money by priorities. That connects, teaches, and inspires.

Small gestures, great adults: when the piggy bank becomes character.

Every big transformation begins quietly, often with a coin dropping into a jar. I remember being around seven. I received my first allowance, and my father gave me a piggy bank and said: "You can spend it all, save it all, or split it. You decide. But afterward, you can't undo it."

That sentence taught me more about financial decisions than any formal course: choice, responsibility, consequence.

Here are two simple stories I often share:

- **Story 1**: Pedro and the video game

Pedro was nine and lived with his mother. He wanted a video game, but it was too expensive to just "receive as a gift."

So his mother proposed: "If you save $5 per week, in two years we'll complete the rest."

Two years feel like forever for a child, but Pedro agreed.

He saved with discipline, cut small extras, learned to say no to friends, and even set aside a small amount to give through a school project. When he reached the goal, it wasn't just a video game. It was a win: self-esteem, patience, proof that time and effort are allies.

- **Story 2:** Isadora and the Christmas bags

Isadora was 11. One day she heard that children in a nearby community would not receive gifts at Christmas, and she had an idea:

- "What if I use my 'give' jar to put together small Christmas bags with candy and toys?"
- With her family's help, she saved over the year in an envelope labeled "Christmas for Good."
- When Christmas arrived, she assembled bags with simple treats, gently used toys, and a handwritten note: "You matter. Merry Christmas."

She learned that money isn't only for buying things, it can create connection, impact, and meaning. And giving isn't losing. It's gaining a different kind of wealth.

When we don't teach, the silence teaches, and it costs.

Kids who never hear healthy money conversations often grow up afraid or ashamed to ask questions.

They learn mainly from marketing, social media, and peers, and may develop limiting beliefs and low tolerance for frustration and delayed results.

When money becomes taboo, people learn through pain, not dialogue. And what's learned through pain creates scars, not wisdom. On the other hand, something beautiful can happen: children can become a positive example inside the home. I've seen parents rethink their habits because their kids became more conscious.

Adults can lead this—even while learning.

Parents, uncles, teachers, caregivers, anyone close to kids can be a financial educator, even if you're learning along the way.

You don't need a degree in economics. You don't need to be an investor. You need willingness: to talk, observe, correct with care, repeat, and live with coherence.

Kids learn little from speeches and a lot from examples. If you feel insecure because you didn't have a strong base, remember:

Admitting you're learning is the best start.

Say something like: "I didn't learn this at your age, but I'm learning now and I want to teach you too."

This teaches humility, shows that learning is continuous, removes the weight of perfection, and helps a child grow with less fear of making mistakes.

Practical actions for adults

Involve children in small decisions (for example, at the grocery store):

- We have $20 for snacks this week. What would you choose with that amount?
- This one is cheaper but smaller. Which is the better value?
- If we save today, we can put money aside to do something fun this weekend.

These simple questions train critical thinking, price awareness, and comparison.

Talk about priorities instead of saying "We don't have money."

If a child asks for something outside the budget, avoid the classic: "We don't have money!"

Try: "This month we chose to use money for your soccer course. Let's see if we can save for that next month."

Or: "We could buy it, but we won't spend on that now because we have other priorities."

This teaches that money is choice, not just limitation.

Create shared goals.

If a child wants something special, a toy, an outing, a party, split the goal: Divide the price, build a simple savings plan together, show progress, celebrate when you reach it.

This teaches that achievement requires effort, but it's possible. It also teaches patience.

Use contribution and anti-waste as part of the lesson.

You can show that collaboration at home can accelerate goals. For example, wasting less food reduces household spending and can help fund a weekend outing or that desired item. It teaches respect for resources and the power of small habits.

Share small wins and small mistakes.

Say lightly: "This week I spent on something unnecessary. I wasn't happy about it. I'll be more careful next time."

Or: "Remember when we saved $10 per week? Today we could do that fun trip because of it."

This shows money isn't shameful. It's part of lifewith mistakes and successes.

If you're an educator, your power is in the routine.

- Use stories and fables about value, trade, and effort.
- Create simple market/bank/planning games.
- Encourage solidarity projects.
- Promote donation drives with active student involvement.
- Create a small "finance club" with real challenges and goals.

Simplicity is the bridge between theory and practice.

Break limiting beliefs early.

Many phrases heard in childhood shape a person for years: "Money is dirty." "Rich people are bad." "Poor people have no choice."

If you heard that, you may have carried it for a long time.

But if you can break the cycle todayand refuse to pass it on, you change the future.

A child who grows up hearing, "You can learn to take care of your money," "Honest work pays," and "Saving today can open doors tomorrow," grows freer, lighter, more prepared.

Plant today what no school can teach tomorrow.

Teaching a child to manage money is the difference between raising an autonomous adult or a dependent adult, between someone who builds and someone who consumes without thinking.

It's an act of love, responsibility, and vision.

Years later, they may not remember the amount of allowance you gave—but they will remember counting coins with you, reaching a goal, turning a "no" into a "yes" after months of saving, and building a "give" jar with their own hands.

They will remember the conversation (in the car, at the market, at the tablE) when they learned money has value, limits, and purpose.

The child you teach today may be the adult who teaches you tomorrow. I've seen it happen.

And it often starts with one simple habit: saving a coin in a jar. You're not only changing their future, you're changing your family's culture. And culture is one of the most powerful assets there are.

Weekly challenge: do this with a child in the next 7 days

Think of one child you know: your child, nephew, grandchild, godchild, student, neighbor.

Choose one simple action to do together. Here are three options:

Challenge 1 — Three jars for the week

- Set up three labeled containers: Spend / Save / Give.
- Provide a symbolic amount ($5, $10, or just coins).
- Let the child decide how to split it.
- Talk about the choices.

Ask: "Why did you put more in that jar?" "What are you saving for?" "How did it feel to give?"

Challenge 2 — Plan a purchase

- Find the price of something they want.
- Define how much to save per week.
- Make a simple progress chart.
- If possible, visit the store and look at the item, without buying yet.

This activates patience, goal setting, and the feeling of achievement.

Challenge 3 — Talk about a mistake (with humility)

- Share a small financial mistake of yours in a light way.
- Explain what you learned (e.g., thinking twice before financing unnecessarily).

This creates a safe space for the child to make mistakes, learn, and grow.

Remember: financial education starts in the piggy bank, but it ends in freedom.

CHAPTER 10

When a credit card becomes a friendly enemy

Freedom That Comes at a Price

When you hear the phrase "friendly enemy," what comes to mind? Someone who hugs you, compliments you, makes you feel safe, while quietly pulling you away from your own strength.

That's how a credit card often behaves.

And let me be clear: I am not saying credit is "bad," and I am not saying credit cards are inherently negative. Credit can be useful. A card can be a tool. The problem is what happens when you don't manage it well. In that case, it can become a very serious problem fast.

Do You Have a Limit, or Does the Limit Have You?

When people say, "I have a card with a $10,000 limit," they usually say it with pride, almost like that limit is part of their net worth. But most people miss the obvious truth: a limit is not a trophy. It is borrowed money that will be collected. With rules. With deadlines. With interest if you get it wrong.

Worse, a high limit can create the illusion that you have more money available than you actually have. And that illusion is where the danger starts.

Human beings spend more when they don't feel the money leaving their hands. Cash creates a small pain: you see it, touch it, feel it. Swiping a card creates no immediate emotional impact. That has a name: emotional disconnection from spending.

The Illusion of Abundance

There's a saying in Portuguese that translates loosely to: "People see the glamorous photo, but they don't see the struggle behind it."

A credit card is a glamorous photo of personal finance. It can hide reality.

Many people walk around with a new phone, a nice watch, branded clothes, expensive dinners, all on credit. But behind the scenes they live in panic, waiting for the statement to arrive.

The card is not the villain for existing. It becomes dangerous when it turns into a mask for a lifestyle you cannot truly support.

And the core issue isn't only financial. It's emotional.

Credit Cards as Modern Anxiety Medication

We live in an era of urgency. We want everything now. We don't want to wait. We don't want to plan. A credit card fits perfectly into that behavior.

Here's a practical example.

Someone wants a new phone. It costs $3,000. They don't have $3,000, but they think: "Ten payments of $300: I can handle that."

They swipe the card, feeling great. Then the next month arrives:

- the phone payment
- the gym membership
- the delivery order they "split into payments"
- the streaming subscriptions
- groceries put on the card "to earn points"

Suddenly, a series of small decisions becomes one big problem. What was supposed to feel like freedom becomes a prison built out of monthly installments.

And what the brain doesn't feel, the wallet pays.

That's why so many people say:

- "I don't even know how I spent that much."
- "It went so fast I didn't feel it."
- "When I looked, my statement was already maxed out."

It's not laziness. It's not stupidity. It's a system designed to make you consume more.

How the Trap Begins

The trap usually starts with small phrases that sound harmless:

- "I'll just finance this one."
- "This month is tight; next month I'll pay everything off."
- "I paid the minimum, but at least I'm not delinquent."
- "Cards are for emergencies... and this is kind of a semi-emergency."
- "I don't want to touch my savings, so I'll put it on credit."

Those sentences don't feel like danger, until they repeat. And repetition turns a habit into a lifestyle.

The Minimum Payment Trap

One of the most expensive lies in personal finance is the idea that paying the minimum is "okay."

Minimum payments often keep you "current," but they push the remaining balance into revolving credit. That's where interest can become brutal. And the longer you carry that balance, the more the debt starts to grow faster than your income.

Here's the math in plain language.

If your statement is $1,200 and you pay only $300:

- you still owe $900
- that $900 starts accumulating interest immediately
- next month, new purchases add on top
- now you are paying interest on yesterday while trying to live today.

This is how people end up working for the statement instead of working for their life.

Signals You Are Losing Control

If any of the points below describes you, take it seriously:

- You pay the minimum frequently.
- You have lost track of how much you truly owe.
- You use credit to cover essentials (groceries,

utilities, rent).
- You avoid looking at the statement until the last minute.
- You have more than two cards and use them all.
- Your limit is higher than your real ability to pay.

None of this makes you a bad person. It just means the tool is controlling you instead of serving you.

What to Do If You Are Already in Trouble

If you are already stuck, you need a plan that is simple and aggressive:

- Stop using the card immediately. No new purchases.
- Calculate the total debt, every card, every balance, every installment.
- Negotiate. If possible, transfer the balance to a lower rate, consolidate, or refinance responsibly.
- Build a payment plan with dates, amounts, and accountability.
- Protect your basics (food, housing, utilities) while you attack the debt.

This is not about shame. It is about clarity. Clarity is what breaks the cycle.

When a Credit Card Can Be a Powerful Ally

A credit card can help you, if you treat it like a tool and not like an extension of your income. Used correctly, it can:

- Help you build credit history
- Provide short-term float with no interest (when you pay in full)
- Give you practical deadlines for cash flow
- Offer fraud protection and safer purchases than carrying cash
- Support budget organization, when tracked daily, not once a month

But these benefits exist only under one condition: you pay in full and you stay in control.

The Emotional Cost

Debt is not only numbers. Debt has symptoms.

You sleep poorly.

You live on alert.

You feel embarrassed to talk to friends.

You fear opening emails or answering calls.

You feel like "I'll never get out of this."

That emotional weight is part of the price.

There is also an emotional limit, not just a financial one. Even if the bank approves a high limit, your nervous system cannot always carry the stress that comes with it.

The 30-Day Reset Challenge

If you need a clean restart, try this:

30 days with no credit card usage.

- During those 30 days, you:
- Reconnect with the real value of money
- Recover the habit of planning
- Avoid unnecessary debt
- Consume with more awareness
- Realize your life doesn't end without installments

For many people, this simple break is the first real step toward freedom.

Rules for Smart Use

If you choose to keep using a credit card, follow strict rules:

- Only use it if the money is already available and set aside.
- Track every expense in real time.
- Follow your statement during the month, not only when it arrives.
- Avoid long installment plans, even "no interest" ones, because they reduce future flexibility.
- Don't keep more than two cards.
- Never use one card to pay another.

**A high limit is not power.
Real power is knowing how to use what
you have with wisdom.**

CHAPTER 11

The "Uberization" of housing and the dream of homeownership

Where Does Your Dream Live?

As long as I can remember, I've heard that "owning a home is every family's biggest dream."

Some phrases sound almost sacred:

- "Once you marry, you need your own place."
- "Better to pay for what's yours than to give money to a landlord."
- "Renting is throwing money away."

" But is that still true? Or are we entering a new era: an era where access is valued more than ownership? An era where a home is less about roots and more about wheels?"

Welcome to the conversation about the "uberization" of housing.

What Does It Mean to "Uberize" a Home?

"Uberize" has become a popular way to describe turning a product into an on-demand service.

Before, you bought a car. Now you call a ride with your phone.

Before, you bought DVDs. Now you stream.

Before, you bought a home and stayed for decades... and now many people prefer to rent, move, and stay flexible.

This mindset is growing among young professionals, digital nomads, single adults with unstable careers, and even older couples who prioritize geographic freedom over fixed stability. It's the logic of mobility: why plant roots if the world keeps moving?

The World That Created the Homeownership Rule Has Changed

The idea of "you must buy a home" was born in a world where:

- Jobs were stable and long-term
- The city where you were born was often where you lived your whole life
- Relationships were expected to last forever
- Inflation could eat rent over time

Today, none of that is guaranteed.

People change careers at 30, 40, 50.

Remote work allows multiple cities.

Many marry later, or don't marry.

Experiences often matter more than possessions.

In this new environment, renting can be a strategy, not a failure.

So... Did the Dream Die?

No. The dream did not die. What changed is the way we relate to it. Before, buying was treated like an obligation.

Today, it should be treated like a strategic decision.

Buying can still be wonderful, but it should never be automatic.

Some people buy without planning, without understanding the real cost, and then spend years "working to pay for bricks."

Others rent out of convenience and never build a plan to accumulate assets, and at 60 they still depend on others.

Balance comes from understanding where you are, what you want, and what the economy allows.

Buy vs. rent is not only emotional. It's math and strategy.

Buy vs. Rent: A Simple Strategic Comparison

Let's remove emotion for a minute and think clearly. Imagine you can either:

- **Option A**: buy a $400,000 home with a 30-year mortgage, put $40,000 down, and pay about $3,500/month or

- **Option B**: rent a similar home for $1,800/month and invest the $40,000 down payment plus the $1,700/month difference.

Over 30 years, with discipline, the investment scenario can surprise you. Depending on returns, the value invested can exceed the total cost of ownership.

"But what if rent rises faster than expected?"

"What if returns are lower than expected?"

"What if the property appreciates above average?"

The honest answer is: there is no single answer.

Everything depends on your profile, discipline, timing, goals, and the quality of your analysis of where and how you invest, or where and how you buy.

A Valuable Warning About Your Money

Remember: your money is the result of your dedication and effort. Even if it came as a gift, an unexpected opportunity, or pure luck, it should be treated as precious: a real blessing.

Only when you treat it as precious will you protect it: refusing "easy promises," avoiding careless decisions, and refusing to trust just anyone with your savings.

When Renting Makes Strategic Sense

There are seasons of life where renting is simply the smartest move:

- Early career, with unstable income
- Professionals who may be transferred or change cities
- People who value freedom, mobility, and simplicity
- Couples without children who are still organizing their finances
- Anyone focused on building capital first

Renting can be a bridge: it keeps you flexible while you build the foundation.

When Buying Can Be the Right Move

Buying can make sense when:

- You have stable income and stable plans
- You expect to stay in the same area long enough to justify transaction costs
- You want to build long-term equity and protect wealth
- You have a healthy down payment and emergency fund
- The total monthly cost fits your budget with margin

Buying can also deliver emotional value:

- A sense of stability,
- Freedom to personalize,
- The feeling of belonging,
- And the comfort of "having a place to return to."

Common Mistakes People Make When Buying

Buying becomes dangerous when you:

- Buy because "everyone is buying"
- Take the maximum loan the bank approves
- Ignore closing costs, taxes, insurance, repairs, and maintenance
- Underestimate how much life can change in 2–5 years
- Treat the house as status instead of strategy

A mortgage is a long-term commitment. Your life must be aligned with that commitment.

A Practical Decision Framework

If you want a clear process, use these steps.

Step 1 — Evaluate your life stage

- "Are you in a growth phase professionally?"
- "Might you move to another city or country?"
- "Do you have children in school and family stability?"
- "Are you professionally established?"
- "Do you see yourself in the same region long-term?"

Step 2 — Analyze your financial situation

- "Do you have an emergency fund?"
- "Is your debt under control?"
- "Can you afford the full cost of ownership (not just the mortgage)?"
- "Do you have the discipline to invest consistently if you choose to rent?"

Step 3 — Do the math on paper

For buying:

- Purchase price
- Down payment
- Mortgage payment
- Rate and total term
- Closing costs, title, recording, taxes
- Insurance and HOA (if applicable)
- Maintenance and repairs
- Realistic appreciation assumptions

For renting + investing:

- Monthly rent
- Difference versus the mortgage scenario
- Realistic investment options for the down payment and monthly difference
- Expected average return (conservative)
- How long you plan to stay in that area

Step 4 — Consider the emotional factor

Ask yourself what a home represents to you:

- Identity and accomplishment?
- Stability for family?
- An emotional anchor for children and spouse?
- A temporary stage in your journey?
- A mobility tool?

Step 5 — Talk to professionals and real people

Speak with:

- A reputable mortgage professional (not a "sales-only" person)

- A financial advisor or planner (fee-based, if possible)
- Homeowners who bought and regret it
- Renters who invested and built wealth

Real stories add realism to your decision.

Your Personal Checklist

Use this checklist as a personal worksheet:

- "Where am I today?"
- "What do I want for the next 5 years?"
- "What is my financial life like right now?"
- "What does a home represent to me?"
- "Scenario A: if I bought today..."
- "Scenario B: if I rented and invested..."

My personal conclusion:

The goal isn't to prove that buying is "right" or renting is "right."
The goal is to choose the path that fits your life, your numbers, and your peace.

CHAPTER 12

Wealth security starts small

The First Stone of the Castle

From an early age, we are taught to desire 'financial security.' But rarely does anyone explain what that truly means. It often sounds like an abstract concept, reserved for people with 'a lot of money' - luxury homes, imported cars, and sophisticated investments.

The truth is different. Building lasting security starts long before wealth - and almost always with something small.

It starts with the first coin you decided to save instead of spend, the first month you ended with $100 more than you began, the first time you understood that saving is as honorable as earning.

Before we go further, let's translate what 'assets' (or 'wealth') means in everyday language, and why it matters so much.

Assets are what you own that create stability, value, or return.

- A home or piece of real estate
- A car (although, in many cases, it behaves more like a liability than an asset)
- Cash savings
- Investments (fixed income or equities)
- A small profitable business
- A solid emergency fund
- Even a collection that appreciates or something you can resell

In short: assets are anything that can support you when your paycheck stops.

Your first property is not always your greatest trophy - it is often your springboard: the beginning, the seed of a tree that, over time, becomes rooted, strong, and large. That is why we call it your first.

Many people wait for the 'perfect' home, in the dream neighborhood, fully furnished, beautifully decorated, close to work.

'The first home is rarely the final one. And that's okay.'

It is a springboard, not a throne. A step. A milestone. A space for learning and growth.

It may be a small financed apartment. It may be land far from downtown. It may be something you buy to rent and generate income. What matters is starting , and turning it into a plan, not a burden. A well-designed life program starts with the right first step, even if it seems small. 'Small' is relative: what looks small to one person can be a dream to another. The ideal size is the one that fits your current season of life in a structured way.

"No fire starts big."

If you still have no assets, or you feel behind, here is the good news: it is not too late. But it is urgent.

Here are simple, realistic ways to take your first steps:

- **Build your emergency fund**: start by saving 10% of everything you earn. Keep it in a separate account, ideally one that earns more than a basic savings account. Touch it only for real emergencies (health, job loss, essential repairs).
- **Invest in low-risk assets:** fixed income, CDs (certificates of deposit), Treasury securities, and other conservative options. Start small, even if it is $100 per month. The point is not the amount - it is the habit.
- **Look for alternative real estate opportunities**: auctions, land in growing areas, pre-construction deals with discounts. Think like an investor, not a consumer.
- **Sell what you do not use anymore and reinvest:** furniture, electronics, branded clothes - turn clutter into capital.
- **Avoid debt that drains your ability to build wealth:** long installments for consumer goods, unnecessary car loans, impulse purchases.

Wealth security is born when you exchange consumption for construction.

Change the Key: From Consumer to Builder

One of the greatest changes you can make for your financial life is to stop being only a consumer, and become a builder.

Consumption can be pleasurable, yes. But building is what will give you freedom in the future.

Security is not in spending well. It is in owning what supports you when you can no longer work the same way.

Your Future Self Will Thank Your Present Discipline

Picture yourself 15 or 20 years from now. "Which sentence would you rather say?"

"I'm glad I started saving, even if it was a little."

"I wish I had started earlier."

The good news is that the choice is still in your hands. Even with a modest income, current debts, and real difficulties, you can start.

Wealth security is not about quantity. It is about consistency, vision, and time.

Starting small is better than not starting. Saving a little is better than staying at zero. Building slowly is infinitely better than living on hope.

The Myths That Keep People From Building Wealth

Now I want to talk about the myths that keep people from taking the first step, and how you can break free.

A supposed 'incapacity' or financial limitation is often the villain that sabotages any attempt to build assets.

Everyone wants assets. But not everyone believes they can have them. And that is the core problem: before you save, you have to believe you can. What you believe about money determines what you do with it.

Here are the main myths that trap millions of people, and how to exit that mindset.

- **Myth 1: 'I don't earn enough to save'**

This is, by far, the most repeated myth in financial conversations. 'How can I save if I barely make it to the end of the month?'

But as time passes, income may even increase... and the person stays at zero. Because the problem is not the amount - it is the behavior.

If you do not save $50 out of $1,000, you will not save $500 out of $10,000. Lifestyle grows with income unless you decide otherwise.

Saving is a habit, not a salary level.

- **Myth 2: 'Saving means depriving yourself of life'**

Many people feel this way: 'So I'm going to save and stop living?' 'I don't even know if I'll be alive tomorrow.' 'I'd rather enjoy now.'

This is 'carpe diem' applied the wrong way. Planning the future is not denying the present. It is ensuring you will have freedom of choice tomorrow.

Security does not mean you stop living. It means you can live better, with less fear.

Everything ends if you do not plan and create a strategy so you do not run out.

- **Myth 3: 'Investing is for rich people'**

How many times have you heard: 'That's for people with a lot of money.' 'That's not for me.'

The truth is that anyone can start. Today, with $30, $50, or $100, you can already invest in conservative products. What is missing is education, not access.

- **Myth 4: 'My only asset is my job'**

Many people confuse income with security. They think a steady paycheck equals safety. But what if you lose your job? Get sick? The company closes? The market changes?

Your job is active income, but it is not an asset. Assets are what remain when income stops.

Real security comes when you have something that supports you beyond your labor.

- **Myth 5: 'It only counts if it's a lot'**

Another common sabotaging thought: 'Saving $50 changes nothing.' 'When I have more, I'll start.'

That mindset prevents discipline. Every big reserve started as a small one. You do not build a house starting with the roof. You start with one brick, then another.

- **Myth 6: 'I have time; I'll organize later'**

This myth is deceptive because it feels calm: 'I'm young; I have time.' 'I'll deal with it later.'

The hard truth is that time is the greatest ally of compound interest. Every year you delay is a year of compounding you will never get back.

The best time to start was yesterday. The second best is today. The worst is leaving it for tomorrow.

The Cure Is Awareness, Decision, and Action

All these myths can be healed, but it requires three steps:

1. Awareness: notice what you believe, where that belief came from, and who taught you.
2. Decision: choose to change, even if it is hard.
3. Action: start with what you have. The amount, the size, the pace - none of that matters as much as starting.

You are not trapped by the myth. You are trapped by continuing to believe it.

If you want security, you must build. To build, you must start. And to start, you must destroy the myths that keep you stuck.

Take real, simple, efficient first steps - even with little, even with fear. Because everything you need to start... you already have.

Six Steps to Make It Work

It does not matter if it is a lot or a little. What matters is taking the first step with clarity, consistency, and courage.

Here is what I call the six steps to make it work:

Step 1 - Create your wealth awareness

Before you save, you need to know where you are. Sit down with paper and pen (or your phone or a spreadsheet) and write:

- How much do you earn (net monthly income)?
- How much do you spend (fixed, variable, and unnecessary expenses)?
- Do you have debt? Which ones? At what rates and terms?
- Do you have any savings? How much? Where?
- Do you own anything that could be considered an asset?

This snapshot is your starting point. Do not panic if the number is negative: the point is to know, so you can act.

Step 2 - Build your emergency fund

Before investing, buying property, or starting a business, build your safety reserve.

A basic guideline:

- For employees: 6 months of fixed monthly expenses
- For self-employed, entrepreneurs, and freelancers: 9 to 12 months

Example: if you spend $3,000 per month to live, an ideal emergency fund is $18,000 to $36,000.

Start with smaller milestones - $1,000, then $3,000, then $6,000. Go step by step, and keep it accessible, safe, and separate.

This fund becomes your springboard for building wealth.

Step 3 - Get out of toxic debt

You cannot build assets while your money leaks through interest. Credit card balances, overdrafts, and high-interest loans will drain you.

Recommended approach:

Make a list of all debts.

- Sort them from highest interest rate to lowest.
- Negotiate, consolidate, or replace with a lower-rate loan when possible.
- Pay the most expensive first (avalanche) or pay the smallest first to build momentum (snowball).
- Every debt you eliminate creates new space to invest.

Step 4 - Create a fixed monthly investment channel

Pick a day of the month - ideally right after you get paid - and transfer your reserved amount to investments.

- Fixed income (Treasuries, CDs, high-quality bonds)
- Mutual funds or index funds
- Retirement accounts (when appropriate)
- REITs or ETFs (for those ready to take market risk)

Do not wait for money to 'be left over.' Make money be left over by treating investing as a priority, not leftovers.

Step 5 - Invest in financial education

You do not have to become an economist. But you must understand enough to avoid being fooled - and to avoid being paralyzed by fear.

Read books. Listen to podcasts. Watch credible experts. Follow people who teach with seriousness. Talk to those who are ahead of you.

Financial education is not expensive. Ignorance is.

A practical suggestion: if this book has helped you, buy another copy and gift it to people you care about. Spread the knowledge as far as you can.

Step 6 - Build the habit, not the hero moment

Many people start by saving $500, get excited... and stop in the third month. Others start with $50, think it is too little... and stop as well. Wealth is built with habit, not impulse. It is like planting a tree: you water it, wait, and trust. In the beginning it seems slow. Later it becomes unstoppable.

The important thing is not how much you start with. It is not stopping.

You do not need to be rich to start. But you must start to have a chance to become rich.

Wealth security is the result of simple decisions repeatedly with discipline. Start today, your way, with what you have.

The Silent Multiplication

Now you understand how to start. Next, understand why

starting as early as possible matters.

Time, when paired with habit, is the most powerful multiplier. It turns drops into an ocean.

Time should always act as your most loyal ally.

Think of an oak seed. In the first years it looks fragile and insignificant. But with time, it becomes a tree that withstands storms. Wealth works the same way.

What you save today - even if it seems small - can become a solid foundation if you respect three laws:

- Consistency - save regularly, even if it is little
- Patience - do not pull out saved money in a hurry
- Good instruments - invest intelligently

You need to understand enough to choose your tools well. Compound interest is one of the secrets you must know.

Compound interest is when the earnings on your money start generating more earnings. In other words: profit generates profit.

A Simple Example

$200 per month invested at 1% per month (about 12.7% per year):

- In 10 years: about $45,000
- In 20 years: about $125,000
- In 30 years: about $290,000

You would have contributed $72,000 - the rest came from time and consistency. Now imagine if it were $400 or $600. Growth is not linear - it is exponential.

Many people make the mistake of withdrawing gains as soon as the investment starts paying. But financial intelligence asks for a different path: reinvest. Let the fruit become seed.

If you earn $50 in returns, reinvest that $50 along with what you would invest that month. This accelerates growth.

Grow with awareness - avoid greed. As you see money grows, the temptation to take bigger risks grows too. That is where many people fall.

Be careful with:

- Promises of fast, high returns
- Pyramid schemes

- Unbacked crypto 'opportunities'
- Anything you do not understand

Growing is good. Growing safely is better. Do not trade consistency for illusion. Hurry can destroy what took years to build.

Another smart move is reinvesting in your ability to generate income. Wealth security is not only about saving. It is also about earning more in a healthy way.

- Skill-building courses
- Certifications
- Intentional networking
- Physical and mental health
- Tools that increase productivity

You are your greatest asset. Taking care of yourself multiplies your invisible wealth and your ability to accumulate visible wealth.

Money does not multiply by magic. It grows with long-term vision, discipline, good choices, reinvestment, and, above all, time.

Starting small is not a limitation - it is intelligence. Whoever learns to multiply $100 with discipline will know what to do when the amounts grow.

Three Real Stories (Names Changed)

One way to internalize these ideas is to learn real stories of people who started small and built something big. Nothing inspires change more than seeing someone like you succeed.

Here are three true stories, adapted with fictional names to protect privacy, but based on real situations.

- Dona Ilda: $10 per week

Dona Ilda worked as a housekeeper for 30 years. She never had a high salary. She had four children and raised them with little help.

But she did one thing consistently: every week she saved $10 in an envelope hidden behind a bookcase. Sometimes $5. Sometimes $20. She never told anyone.

At 56, when she was laid off and thought everything was over, she opened her reserve and realized she had enough to breathe and reorganize. She built wealth with envelopes and discipline.

- Rafael: from debt to freedom

Rafael, 29, a systems analyst, was living with heavy debt. He had a financed car, installment payments on everything, and a lifestyle built on delivery food, branded clothes, and weekend parties.

After a health scare and a conversation with a mentor, he decided to change. He created an aggressive payoff plan, cut expenses, and started investing what was left.

Four years later:

- He paid off all his debts
- He has $85,000 invested
- He lives alone in a rented apartment with a strategic rent choice
- He saves 35% of his monthly income
- He has freedom of choice

What changed? Mindset. Priorities. Habit.

- Silvana: invisible investing

Silvana is a teacher. She was always disciplined but never had big ambitions. She started saving $200 per month as soon as she began teaching. She did not know much about investing, so she chose conservative options. After 10 years, she realized she had more than $35,000 saved. That is when she sought guidance and diversified. Today, at 45:

- She has a modest but comfortable paid-off apartment
- She has more than $140,000 in investments
- She still teaches - but by choice, not necessity
- She is taking a course to open a private early-childhood school

She never earned a lot, but she never spent as if she had everything. That is what assets are: freedom of choice.

These stories are not about how much someone earns. They are about how much someone saves with discipline.

You may not identify with every detail, but you carry a piece of each: persistence, the ability to change, and the power of consistency.

You can be one of these stories. Your name may not be in the headlines yet. But your wealth begins in the quiet decisions.

Exercise: Your Personal Wealth Map

I propose one more exercise: a personal wealth mapping - an

honest snapshot of what you have, what you can build, and what you need to change. Because your castle may simply be waiting for you to place the first stone.

Knowledge only becomes transformation when it turns into action. So, grab paper and pen (or a notes app or spreadsheet) and let's build your first wealth plan.

Part 1 - An X-ray of today

Be brutally honest with yourself. Write:

- Net monthly income (what truly comes in):
- Fixed monthly expenses (rent, bills, transportation, basic food):
- Variable expenses and lifestyle (delivery, entertainment, clothes, etc.):
- Open debts (amounts, terms, and rates):
- How much is left over (or missing) each month:
- Do you have any savings? Where? What does it earn?
- Do you own anything with asset value (property, land, car, funds, CDs, etc.)?

This is your real starting photo. No filters. No judgment.

Part 2 - Where do you want to go?

Answer honestly:

- ***What is your dream of financial security? (Example: a paid-off home, living off investments, the ability to stop working early.)***
- ***How much wealth would you like to have in the next 1 year?***
- ***In the next 3 years?***
- ***In the next 10 years?***
- ***What is the ideal size of your emergency fund?***
- ***What is a realistic amount to save per month in your current situation?***
- ***Are you willing to cut any expenses in exchange for future stability? Which one?***

Remember: there is no single right answer. There is what is right for you.

Part 3 - A plan you can execute and adjust

Now design a simple but realistic action plan:

- Amount you will save every month starting with your next paycheck:
- Where will you keep it (institution and product):
- Fixed day of the month you will transfer it (preferably automated):
- Goal for this money (emergency fund, down payment, retirement, etc.):
- Monthly review: on the same day each month, will you review your progress - yes or no?

The secret is consistency, not perfection. A powerful extra tip is to visualize and track your progress. Use a notebook, a wall chart, a spreadsheet with graphs, or an app. Watch the balance grow. Celebrate progress. When you see your wealth growing, even slowly, your brain commits to the process. You leave the scarcity mindset and enter the building cycle. And that changes everything.

Final Reprogramming

Say to yourself:

- “I am capable of building my wealth.”
- “I do not depend on luck; I depend on action.”
- “I respect myself enough to take care of my future.”
- “Small steps are better than big excuses.”

Repeat it. Believe it. Do it.

You do not need to be a specialist. You just need to be consistent.

Wealth begins with the invisible - in the idea, the belief, the choice. But it becomes visible with time, habit, and clarity.

If you follow this path, even if it feels slow, one day you will look back and realize you built a fortress where there used to be fear.

‘I am secure. Because I stayed faithful to myself.’

CHAPTER 13

You are your greatest active income source

The Asset No One Can Take Away From You

Get ready: I am going to help you dive into one of the most transformative points in this book - the value of your ability to generate income from what you know, what you do, and what you learn. You will discover that investing in yourself is the most profitable asset of all.

When most people hear the word 'investments,' they think of:

- Real estate
- Stocks
- Funds
- Fixed income
- Businesses

Few people think of themselves. And that is exactly where the secret is for those who grow consistently: they understand that their greatest asset is themselves.

The Value-Generating Machine

Imagine you have a machine at home. It runs eight hours a day. It produces something that can be sold on the market. The better you maintain it, the more it earns.

Now understand: that machine is you. Your body. Your mind. Your energy. Your ability to learn, produce, sell, serve, and think.

Everything you earn today is the result of your performance - as an employee, freelancer, business owner, or creator. You are the source of your active income.And the more you develop, the more value you generate. Investing in yourself is simple: it is dedicating time, effort, and resources to become more skilled, healthier, more productive, and more creative.

Examples:

- **Study**: take courses, learn new skills, read technical or inspiring books
- **Practice**: apply what you learn, test ideas, seek feedback
- **Care for your body:** health is capital. Better sleep, nutrition, and energy increase output
- **Care for your mind**: manage emotions, build emotional intelligence, keep clarity
- **Connect:** build relationships, participate in groups, build reputation
- **Create or build:** turn ideas into solutions, solve problems, deliver value

All of that is investment. And the return comes as higher income, opportunities, recognition, and freedom.

Your Active Income Can Grow With You

Stop and ask yourself: "What I earn today - is it more connected to my effort, or to my development?"

Most people trade time for money. They work for an hourly wage, a delivery, a salary. But the people who grow the most learn to increase their value per hour.

That happens through:

- More specialized knowledge
- The ability to solve more complex problems
- Relationships that open bigger doors
- Differentiation that makes you unique

A resume can say a lot. But your posture, your delivery, and your constant evolution say more. Beware of the comfort trap. Many people stop growing because:

- They already have a 'good' job
- They feel they have learned enough
- They believe studying is only for those who are 'starting out'

But the market changes. Demands change. Technology

accelerates. Whoever does not invest in themselves today is preparing to become irrelevant tomorrow. Staying in motion is the only maintenance plan.

You are the greatest source of value in your financial life. No matter how much you have in the bank, what you know and do can create, multiply, and protect your income.

The best investment is the one that walks with you, lives with you, and grows with you: yourself.

Identify Your Skills and Turn Them Into Value

After you understand that you are your greatest asset, the next step is to look inward and map your abilities. You may think you have none, or that what you know cannot generate income. That is rarely true.

Do this exercise now:

- "What do you do well (even if it seems simple)?" Example: spreadsheets, cooking, explaining things, fixing, listening, organizing.
- "What do people always ask you for help with?" Example: advice, reviews, explanations, recommendations.
- "What do you enjoy doing and would do even for free?" Example: drawing, researching, planning, sewing, writing.
- "What have you learned in life that you could teach?" Example: overcoming challenges, lived experience, personal methods.
- Everything can be refined. Turning skill into value starts with recognizing it.

After you identify your abilities, the next step is converting them into income - as a service, product, or solution.

Possible paths:

- **Direct service**: offer what you can do as a professional or freelancer
- **Classes or mentoring:** teach what you know (online or in person)
- **Digital content**: creating videos, posts, or courses that educate

- **Products**: crafts, design, writing, organizing, consulting,
- **Use it inside your current job**: propose improvements, lead projects, pursue promotions based on new skills.

Start small. One class per week. A side project. A new course. The key is getting your skill out of your head and into the world.

Example: you like sewing. You start making bags. The first ones do not sell. You improve finishing and design. In the third batch, you sell five, then ten. Soon you have a brand.

This applies to everything: video editing, financial coaching, baking, copyediting, personal training - the list is endless.

Use technology in your favor.

Today you do not need a storefront, an office, or heavy upfront investment. You need a first offer and the courage to test.

- Sell on Instagram, WhatsApp, or marketplaces
- Take free or affordable online courses
- Promote your work in local groups
- Use tools like Canva, ChatGPT, Google Docs, and Trello to increase productivity

The internet democratized access. But your attitude determines whether you enter the game. Do not confuse talent with destiny.

Phrases like 'I don't have that,' 'some people were born with it,' or 'I'm not creative' sabotage your evolution. Skill is training. It is repetition. It is exposure.

Everyone you admire was once a beginner. You just do not see the early stage.

Inside you there is a spark of value that can be accessed, trained, and turned into results.

Body, Mind, and Energy: The Foundation of Your Income

Building yourself goes beyond knowledge or credentials. You must learn how to care for your body, your mind, and your energy. And believe it: your financial side is directly connected to that care.

Physical, mental, and emotional health is fuel for productivity, clarity, and consistency - a tripod for growth.

Body, mind, and energy are your most precious resources.

"What is the point of talent, knowledge, and opportunity if you have no strength to act?" Your body is your vehicle. Your mind is your command center. Your energy is your fuel.

When your mind is tired, anxious, or stressed, you:

- **Procrastinate**
- **Make impulsive decisions**
- **Miss opportunities out of fear or disorganization**
- **Cannot see what is working**
- **Self-sabotage through insecurity**

A suffering brain does not think about growth; it thinks about survival. That is why mental health is not luxury - it is strategy.

Practices to keep your mind healthy:

- Protect real rest and sleep. Sleeping poorly is like fueling with contaminated gas - performance drops.
- Reduce digital overload. Excess time on social media drains attention, fuels comparison, and consumes creative energy.
- Talk about what you feel. Therapy, mentoring, support groups, trusted friends - carrying everything alone is heavy.
- Have moments of leisure and purpose: walking, music, cooking, serving, prayer , anything that reconnects you to what matters.

Caring for your mind makes space for new ideas to bloom.

Your body also needs to be strong. You need it to work, create, decide, and execute. There is no 'rich version' of a weak body.

You do not need to be an athlete. But you must respect your body as your instrument in the world.

A neglected body equals lost energy. A cared-for body equals renewed energy.

Minimum self-care habits are not optional. Building a healthy body is also financial discipline.

- Eat real food: less ultra-processed, more whole foods
- Move: a 20-minute walk a day changes mood and energy
- Breathe deeply several times a day to oxygenate the brain and calm the nervous system
- Avoid constant excess: alcohol, sugar, screens, sedentary life
- Do annual checkups: prevention is cheaper than treatment

Health is an invisible investment that pays dividends as well-being, focus, and productive longevity.

Energy matters too. Have you met someone who 'lifts the room' and someone who 'drains it'? That is energy. And it affects relationships, clients, and opportunities.

This Triad Sustains Your Active Income
•Healthy body -> stamina, presence, resilience
•Clear mind -> focus, decisions, creativity
•Good energy -> relationships, sales, confidence

You can be technically brilliant, but if you are exhausted, anxious, and bitter, people will not want to work with you. You are not a work machine. You are a whole person - body, mind, and soul. The better you treat yourself, the more you produce.

Your Network Multiplies Your Income

Active income is not only individual effort. It is also knowing how to surround yourself with the right people. Your network amplifies your talent.

You have heard 'out of sight, out of mind.' In the real world of income, it becomes: if you are not visible, you are not remembered.

Your resume can open doors. But your reputation and the people who know you create opportunities.

Networking is not about 'having many friends.' It is about having a few strategic, trustworthy connections.

Build your network authentically:

- Be useful before you expect anything: help without immediate demands; reputation grows.
- Share knowledge: teach, post, comment, answer questions; it positions you as someone who knows.
- Do not reject invitations automatically: sometimes an informal coffee becomes a partnership.
- Use online spaces wisely: LinkedIn, professional groups, webinars. Being online is not enough - being active and intentional.
- Nurture old relationships: former colleagues, classmates, past managers, neighbors. A few check-ins per year keep bridges alive.

Network ethics matter. This is not a dirty game. Partnerships work only when they are honest and mutually beneficial.

You are not an island. Your talent matters, but your presence, visibility, and network often matter even more.

Do Not Fly With One Wing: Build Multiple Income Streams

Pursuing income is essential. Increasing income is indispensable for growth. But sometimes growth is not only about earning more; it is about reducing dependence.

Depending on a single income source is like flying with one wing. If it fails - a job loss, a client who disappears - you crash.

The good news is that you can build two, three, or five income streams using what you already know, or by learning. Before thinking 'get rich,' think 'get protected.' Diversification is safety.

Examples of small 'income satellites' that can orbit your main income:

- One private lesson per week
- Editing work on weekends
- An informal consultation for friends
- A product you know how to make
- Content that can generate income later
- A course sold on an online platform

Analyze your human capital - you. When you understand what you are made of, you see how and where to expand.

Practical steps:

List your skills and interests. What do you do well and enjoy?

1. Look for demand in your circle. Are people asking for help? Paying others for something you can do?
2. Test small deliveries. Do not wait to be 100% ready. Offer something simple: a class, a tip, a session.
3. Price and improve. Charge low at first, but deliver quality. Adjust as you grow.
4. Use existing platforms and channels (marketplaces, social media, local communities) to find your first customers.

The extra income cycle is powerful: extra income creates more security. Security reduces fear. With less fear, you make better decisions.

It all starts with a simple question: 'What else can I offer the world with what I already know?'

You do not need to become a business owner to have multiple income streams. You just need to accept that you know something that can be valuable.

Exercise

Part 1 - Your current snapshot

Grab a sheet of paper, a notebook, a notes app, or a spreadsheet. Answer honestly:

- What is your main income today (salary, pension, commissions, etc.)?
- Where does it come from? (full-time job, freelance, occasional services?)
- Do you depend exclusively on that source?
- Do you currently have any complementary income (even small)?
- What is your biggest practical skill or knowledge today?

Part 2 - Inventory of talents and possibilities

Think: 'If I needed to generate $500 more this month using what I know, how would I do it?'

List:

- Three skills or talents you have (teaching, organizing, video editing, baking, writing, etc.)

- Two things people always ask for your help with or compliment you on
- One thing you would do for free because you truly enjoy it

Reflect: "Is there a format in which I can offer this as a product, service, or paid help?"

Part 3 - A 30-day test plan

Based on your list, create a simple test plan:

- Which skill will you test as an income source in the next four weeks?
- For whom? (who can be your first client?)
- How will you offer it? (Instagram, WhatsApp, word of mouth, a flyer, a community group, etc.)
- How many hours per week can you dedicate?
- What would be a fair starting price (even symbolic)?

Example:

- Skill: organizing small homes
- First client: a cousin who lives alone
- Format: offer one free day of organizing in exchange for a social post and referrals
- Goal: get at least one paying client by the end of the month

Simple. Practical. Possible.

Part 4 - Visualize your evolution

Now imagine three months from today. If you do this every week, what will you have gained?

- More confidence
- More financial returns
- More clarity of direction
- More proof that you have value
- And, most importantly, the certainty that you do not depend only on a job, a boss, or luck

You depend on you - and you are becoming stronger.

You depend on you - and you are becoming stronger.

Part 5 - Make a commitment to yourself

To finish, write this sentence in your notebook (yes, actually write it) or wherever you can read it:

> **"Starting today, I recognize that I am my greatest source of income.**
> **Everything I will build starts with me - what I know, what I learn, and what I deliver to the world.**
> **And I commit to developing myself, caring for myself, and valuing myself every day as my greatest investment."**
> **Sign it. Add the date. Take a photo and save it as a reminder of where your turning point began.**

You are your biggest project. Your greatest capital. Your greatest investment.

Take care of yourself, study, move, deliver value to the world - and life will pay you back with abundance.

Let's transform dreams into concrete goals by creating a personal and financial growth plan with clarity, direction, and deadlines. Because what is not measured does not improve. And who does not plan only hopes.

CHAPTER 14

How to make money work for you

The goal of this chapter is to help you flip the switch, from being an employee of money to becoming an owner of capital. I want to show you that you must learn how to use money so it can grow beyond its face value. It can sound complex, but by the end you will see that simple concepts, applied with consistency, can multiply what you produce with your work. We are going to use what often feels like an enemy, compound interest, in your favor.

When I was younger, I thought the secret to stability was simple: earn well and spend less. That is the foundation. But over the years I realized something even more powerful:

"Financial freedom starts when you stop chasing money... and make money start chasing you."

Money was not made only to be spent. Money can work.

Just like you have a workday, money can have one too, if you put it in the right role.

What does "making money work" really mean?

It is not just a nice phrase. It means the money you earn continues to generate more money even when you are not actively working. When allocated well, it multiplies over time. It produces returns: interest, dividends, distributions, price appreciation, like a reliable employee. You stop trading only "time for money" and you start earning from what you accumulated and invested. That is the difference between working for money and having money work for you.

Picture of two people:

- Marcos earns $10,000 a month, spends it all, and depends entirely on his paycheck.
- Rita earns $5,000 a month and invests $1,000 every month with intention.

A few years later:

- Marcos still has a strong income, but he is exhausted and trapped in the routine. If he stops working, the money stops.
- Rita, through discipline, built a portfolio that generates $2,000 a month. If she needs to pause, money still comes in.

Marcos works for money.

Rita makes money work for her.

And the most interesting part?

Rita did not need to earn more than Marcos; she simply learned the game earlier.

Time is the secret, not the starting amount.

Many people believe investing is "only for people with a lot of money." That is false. The greatest ally of an investor is not the initial deposit: it is time and consistency.

Whoever starts small, but early and disciplined, often harvests more than someone who starts late with a big amount. Because compound interest, the real engine of multiplication, needs time.

Imagine investing $200 per month for 20 years with an average annual return of 10%.

At the end, you will have contributed $48,000...

But the total can be close to $140,000.

You did not earn that extra amount by working more hours. You earned it because your money worked for you. Next month's return is calculated on your original principal plus the gains that stayed invested. The percentage return may be the same, but the dollar amount grows because the base grows. That is why leaving the gains invested matters.

Think of it like a pomegranate: the seeds support each other. The more they multiply, the bigger the fruit becomes. Gains join principal—interest on interest.

In this "math magic," the key is to make the result work for you as profit, not against you as debt.

A simple example:

- You invest $1,000 at 10% per year.
- Year one: you earn $100.
- Year two: you earn 10% on $1,100, not on $1,000.
- Over time, it accelerates.

What grows the most is not what you put in it, it's what it produces and reinvests. People love to quote Einstein calling compound interest "the eighth wonder of the world." Whether or not he said it, the idea is true: compound growth rewards patience.

Before you invest, you must save, with intention.

The first step starts when you save instead of spending. It becomes real when you save on purpose. It is not "saving what is left over." It is reserving something as soon as you get paid, like a non-negotiable commitment.

Even if it is $50 a month and it feels small, what matters is starting. And that money cannot sit idle in a checking account. It needs a destination. Now you enter the world of investing.

Up to now you may have worked too hard for money, chasing income, paying down debts, adjusting bills. But now it is time to flip the game: give every dollar a mission, grow, earn, protect, and build freedom.

So where do you put your money first?

The good news is there are simple, accessible ways to start in the U.S.

The bad news is that without understanding, people fall into traps.

Knowledge comes before investing.

Below are common paths for beginners; explained in a way that helps you start with clarity.

1) U.S. Treasuries: the "base layer" of safety

U.S. Treasury securities are loans to the federal government. They are generally considered among the safest instruments in the market.

Common options include:

- Treasury Bills (T-Bills): short-term (weeks to 1 year). Often useful for short goals and cash management.
- Treasury Notes and Bonds: longer maturities (2+ years).
- Inflation-protected Treasuries (TIPS): designed to help protect purchasing power over time.

In practice, many people use Treasury options—directly (via TreasuryDirect) or through a brokerage or fund—as part of an emergency fund or as a conservative layer of a portfolio.

2) High-yield savings accounts and CDs: you lend to the bank

A high-yield savings account (HYSA) pays interest while keeping money available.

A Certificate of Deposit (CD) is similar, but usually requires leaving money for a set term.

Key points:

- Often pay more than traditional savings accounts.
- Some CDs have early-withdrawal penalties—read the terms.
- In the U.S., FDIC insurance typically protects deposits up to $250,000 per depositor, per insured bank, per ownership category.

The lesson is the same as always: higher promised returns usually require either time, risk, or limits on access. If you might need the money soon, prioritize liquidity.

3) Mutual funds and ETFs: diversification made simple

A mutual fund or ETF (exchange-traded fund) pools investors' money and buys a basket of assets: stocks, bonds, or both.

Why does it help beginners:
- You diversify without having to pick individual securities.
- Professional management (mutual funds) or rules-based exposure (many ETFs).
- You can start with small amounts, especially with fractional shares.

Pay attention to costs. Fees matter. Over decades, a "small" annual expense ratio can consume a lot of returns.

4) REITs: real estate exposure without buying property

REITs (Real Estate Investment Trusts) are companies that own or finance income-producing real estate. You can buy REIT shares or REIT funds.

They can provide:
- Exposure to real estate and cash-flow distributions.
- Liquidity (publicly traded REITs can be sold like stocks).

Important note: in the U.S., REIT distributions are often taxable in a regular brokerage account (though holding them in retirement accounts can change the tax impact). Always understand what you own and how it is taxed.

5) Stocks: ownership in businesses

When you buy a stock, you become a shareholder in a company. Stocks can be volatile in the short term, but they have historically played a central role in long-term wealth building. You may benefit through price appreciation and dividends.

This requires more emotional discipline and a longer time horizon. Stocks are generally not ideal for money you will need soon.

6) **Other common tools in the U.S.**

- Employer retirement plans (401(k), 403(b), etc.): especially powerful when there is an employer match.
- IRAs (Traditional or Roth): tax-advantaged accounts for retirement goals.
- Money market funds: often used for short-term cash management (they are investments, not bank deposits).
- Cryptoassets: extremely volatile—only for those who study and only with money they can afford to lose.
- Alternative investments: may exist, but are typically for more advanced profiles.

There is no single "best investment."
There is the best option for you—based on:

- Your goal (short, medium, long term)
- Your risk tolerance
- Your need for liquidity
- Your knowledge and ability to stay calm

The best approach is usually balance:
safety, return, and access.

The Investor Ladder: build wealth one step at a time

Wealth is built like climbing a staircase: one step at a time.
Investing is not jumping off a cliff hoping you can fly. It is

climbing with stability, where each step is a real achievement. You can start simple, but you do not need to stop there.

Here is a practical five-step ladder:

Step 1 — Save with discipline

Before thinking about returns, you need something to invest. This step is about:

- Creating the habit of saving a fixed amount every month
- Building your emergency fund
- Reaching your first $1,000 through effort—not shortcuts

Automate it. Set an automatic transfer the day you get paid. Turn discipline into a quiet habit.

Step 2 — Build your base with liquid, low-risk options

This is where many people use:

- High-yield savings accounts
- Money market funds
- Short-term Treasuries (like T-Bills)

The goal is stability, not "spectacular returns."

Step 3 — Longer-term fixed income for defined goals

Once you have an emergency fund, you can pursue better rates with time:

- CDs with longer terms
- Bond funds or Treasuries with longer maturities
- Inflation-protected options (like TIPS), depending on your objectives

Here, time starts working for you.

Step 4 — Diversified funds and real estate exposure

Now you diversify more intentionally:

- Broad stock/bond funds
- Target-date or balanced funds (if appropriate)
- REITs or REIT funds for real-estate exposure

At this stage, you start to feel your money "working" while you sleep.

Step 5 — Stocks and more advanced allocations

Here you can explore:

- Individual stocks (with study and restraint)
- Broad equity ETFs
- Sector exposure (with caution)
- Small allocations to highly volatile assets only if you understand the risks

At this step, you invest not because you "want to get rich fast," but because you understand what you are doing and you can stay consistent.

Ask yourself: which step are you on?

You do not need to be at the top. But you must be on the staircase. Staying off the ladder is what keeps money idle—and idle money loses value over time.

Sometimes you may climb too fast, invest aggressively, and realize you cannot sleep. That is okay. Step back and reorganize. The goal is not to "look like a successful investor." The goal is peace and consistency. Common mistakes that stop money from working,

Money often "runs away" before it ever starts working—because of avoidable mistakes.

- **Mistake 1 — Investing without an emergency fund**

Without a reserve, one flat tire, a medical bill, or a job interruption can force you to sell investments at the worst time.

What to do: Build a 3–6 month emergency fund in a liquid, low-risk place first (HYSA, money market, short-term Treasuries). Then climb.

- **Mistake 2 — Chasing trends and strangers' tips**

The "friend who doubled his money" story is everywhere. So are influencers promising quick gains.

Investing is not gambling. It is a life plan.

Before investing, you should understand at least:

- What you are buying
- The risks
- The time horizon
- The purpose

If it sounds too good to be true, treat it as a red flag.

- **Mistake 3 — Ignoring fees, taxes, and lockups**

A return that looks great on paper can shrink after:

- Fund fees
- Advisory fees
- Taxes
- Penalties for early withdrawals

Always read the terms. Compare options. Cost matters.

- **Mistake 4 — Putting everything in one place**

Concentration is fragile. Diversification is a core principle of disciplined investing.

Even with small amounts, you can spread exposure across categories and time horizons.

- **Mistake 5 — Investing money, you will need soon.**

If you will need the money next month for rent, tuition, or a car payment, it does not belong in volatile or long-term investments. Put short-term money where it stays accessible.

- **Mistake 6 — Quitting after the first downturn**

Markets move. A temporary decline is normal.

Panic selling turns normal volatility into permanent loss.

Invest only in what you can leave invested for years, and keep your emotions in check.

- **Mistake 7 — Wanting to get rich fast**

This is the most dangerous trap. Scammers feed on impatience. If someone promises guaranteed returns well above the market with "no risk," run.

Whenever possible, verify whether a firm or professional is registered with U.S. regulators (such as the SEC and FINRA) and be cautious with anything that avoids transparency.

A personal investment plan: from concept to action

Now let's turn this into a plan that fits your reality—your income, your limits, your goals.

Stage 1 — Your current snapshot
Answer honestly (write it down):

- "What is your average monthly take-home pay?"
- "What are your essential fixed monthly expenses?"
- "How much can you save per month today?"
- "Do you have an emergency fund? If yes, how many months of expenses?"
- "Do you already invest? Where and how much?"

This is your starting point. No judgment—just clarity.

Stage 2 — Define your goals
List at least three goals with timeframes and estimated amounts.
Example:

- Replace your car in 2 years ($30,000)
- Down payment on a home in 5 years ($80,000)
- A comfortable retirement in 25 years ($500,000+)

Dream—but attach a timeline, a number, and a plan.

Stage 3 — Create a simple allocation strategy
As a starting framework:

- Emergency fund (3–6 months): HYSA / money market / short-term Treasuries
- Short term (0–2 years): T-Bills, short CDs, conservative bond funds
- Medium term (3–5 years): a mix of bonds/funds and, if appropriate, limited equity exposure

- Long term (10+ years): diversified stock/bond funds, retirement accounts, broad equity ETFs

Start small, but start correctly.

Stage 4 — A first monthly plan (example)
If you can invest $200 per month, that is enough to begin.

Example allocation:
- $100 to your emergency-fund base (HYSA or short-term Treasuries)
- $60 to a diversified fund (broad index ETF or balanced fund)
- $40 to a longer-term goal bucket (CD ladder, bond fund, or retirement account)

Adapt to your situation. The key is having a plan and following it.

Stage 5 — Review rhythm
Decide:
- When you invest (e.g., the day after payday)
- Where you track it (broker app, spreadsheet, budgeting app)
- When you review (every 3 months is a good start)

Consistency matters more than chasing "amazing returns."

Stage 6 — Your personal commitment
Write this as a personal contract:

**"Starting today, I commit to investing part of my income every month,
with awareness, patience, and a long-term view.
I understand my future freedom
depends on the choices I make now.
I will study, adjust, and persist,
because my money must work for me, not the other way around."
Sign it. Date it. Keep it somewhere private—but visible enough to remind you when you manage your finances.**

You made it here with something many people do not have: awareness and the will to change.

Your plan does not need to be perfect. It needs to exist—and it needs to be executed.

A year from now, you will be grateful you started today.

And you will smile when you realize that, even slowly, your money is finally working, and you are closer to freedom.

CHAPTER 15

Clear goals, clear finances

This chapter is fundamental because it teaches you how to turn dreams into tangible financial objectives, with timelines, strategy, and emotional discipline. The point is to bring clarity to your financial journey, because when you do not know where you want to go, you accept any road, and any expense.

Let's begin with one of the most powerful keys to financial transformation: clarity. This is not just about earning more or spending less. It is about knowing exactly why and for what purpose you are doing both.

If you don't know what you want, you buy what you don't need

"Why are you saving?"

I asked that question once to a coworker who, every payday, did the ritual of cutting "extras."

- Coffee out? Cut.
- Streaming subscription? Canceled.
- Weekend restaurant? Just look at the menu.

And even with all that, he stayed frustrated.

He could not save as much as he wanted.

And he didn't even know why.

Then it clicked: he was saving out of obligation, not purpose.

And when saving has no objective, it becomes sacrifice.
Sacrifice without meaning is quickly abandoned.

Financial goals should be lighthouses, not chains.

When you hear "financial goals," what do you feel first?
Tired? Pressured? Afraid of being disappointed?
If so, understand this: goals are not there to imprison you. They exist to guide you.
They are lighthouses in the ocean of consumption.
Without them, any wave—discounts, desire, impulse—pushes you off course.

Without a goal, your money loses direction

Imagine getting into a taxi, sitting in the back, and saying only: "Go." The driver looks at you, confused:

- *"Where to?"*
- *"I don't know... just go."*

It sounds ridiculous, but it is what many people do with their money. They spend it here, invest there, save a little—without direction.
After years of effort, they have no idea where the money went. Clarity brings peace. Clarity brings power.
Every time someone asks me:
"Where do I start improving my financial life?"
I answer with another question:
"What do you want to achieve in the next three years?"

Because that answer changes everything.
It helps you:

- Prioritize what matters
- Say "no" to distractions without guilt
- Know where to put the money you save
- Measure real progress

A goal begins with three characteristics

A financial goal needs to be:

- **1) Clear**

"Save money" is not a goal.
"Save $12,000 for a car down payment by next December" is.

- **2) Measurable**

If you can't measure it, you can't manage it.
You must be able to track the numbers month by month.

- **3) Time-bound**

A goal without a deadline is a wish.
Time forces focus.

Examples of clear goals

Short-term achievements:

- Pay off a credit-card balance by a specific date
- Build a $1,500 emergency starter fund
- Pay for a trip in cash instead of financing it
- Save for a course, certification, or career transition

Medium-term goals:

- Replace a car without going into debt
- Save a down payment for a home
- Build a savings cushion for a child's education or family plans
- Create a small investment portfolio that generates an extra monthly income

Long-term goals:

- Financial independence
- A comfortable retirement
- A paid-off home
- Leaving a legacy instead of leaving debts

If money is your effort materialized, the goal is the meaning of that effort. Having goals is not being rigid. It is being intentional.

It is stopping the "improvisation lifestyle."

It is saying: *"I know what I want, and I am moving toward it."*

The three stations of the journey: short, medium, and long term

A well-structured financial life looks like a travel map.

A map needs landmarks—stops along the way—and clarity about destination and route.

- **Short term (0–12 months)**

These are immediate, tangible goals. They have a known cost and a direct impact on your daily life.

Examples:

- Create an emergency fund starter amount
- Pay off a specific debt
- Build a "buffer" so you stop living paycheck to paycheck

Strategy:

Keep short-term money liquid and stable. Your priority here is access and safety, not high returns.

- **Medium term (1–5 years)**

This is where planning becomes visible. These goals require consistency and better organization.

Examples:

- Down payment for a home
- Career investment (education, licensing, equipment)
- Building a meaningful savings cushion

Strategy:

Choose a mix that balances safety and growth, aligned with when you will need the money.

- **Long term (5+ years)**

This is the land of patience.Where compound growth and consistency can transform your future.

Examples:

- Retirement
- Financial independence
- Building wealth for family, business, or legacy

Strategy:

Use long-term vehicles and diversification. Time is your partner here, but only if you stay invested and keep contributing.

How to set goals that you actually follow

A goal you don't review becomes invisible.
A goal you don't break down becomes overwhelming.

- **Here is a practical method:**

1) Pick one "North Star"
Your main goal for the next 3 years.
Write it clearly, with a number and a date.

2) Break it into quarterly milestones
What must be true in 90 days to be on track?

3) Break it into monthly actions
How much must you save or invest per month?

4) Make it visible
Put it somewhere you will see your planner, your phone notes, your budgeting app.

5) Track progress like a professional
If you're 10% behind, adjust the plan: not your identity.
You're not "bad with money." You're learning.

Goals need emotional alignment

Many people fail not because the goal was wrong, but because it didn't connect to their heart.

Ask yourself:

- *"Why is this goal important to me?"*
- *"What will change in my life if I achieve it?"*
- *"Who benefits when I become financially stronger?"*
- *"What pain am I trying to avoid repeating?"*

When the "why" is strong, discipline becomes lighter.

Your environment matters

Financial progress is not just a personal decision. The people around you influence your habits, your spending, and your emotional stability.

If you want a stronger financial life, bring the people closest to you into the conversation, especially your spouse, partner, or family.

Shared vision reduces conflict.

Clear goals reduce anxiety.

A plan brings unity.

There is an old story: a frog told a pig that the farmer's son was getting married and that an animal might be slaughtered for the celebration. The frog suggested warning the ox so the ox could stay out of sight in the pasture and avoid being chosen. The pig decided not to share the warning and kept the information to himself.

The next morning, the farmer saw the ox grazing slowly. The ox was too large for a small celebration. The farmer then told the farm manager to go to the barn and bring the pig—the pig had been quiet and looked heavy enough for the feast.

The lesson is simple: knowledge shared can create a chain of wins. Sometimes protecting only yourself is what puts you most at risk.

Include the people you love in your growth.

Your success is connected to the success of those around you—and vice versa.

In the end, building financial education is more than learning "about money."

It is understood that money decisions support a life with peace, health, and meaningful experiences—where dreams are planned, achieved, and celebrated.

And that is why clarity matters.

Clear goals create clear finances.
Clear finances create a clearer life.

CHAPTER 16

The economic reality and you

Why the World Matters to Your Wallet

When you hear words like "inflation," "interest rates," "the dollar," or "global markets," it can sound like a distant universe reserved for economists, banks, and big investors. But the truth is simple: that universe shows up in your life every day.

Every time groceries cost more, a loan payment increases, or your job market feels uncertain, there are economic forces behind it, and you can understand enough of them to act instead of reacting.

When the tide goes out, you see who's been swimming naked.— Warren Buffett.

That line captures a principle: when the economy tightens, it reveals who was not prepared.

You don't need to become a specialist, but you do need to understand the economy around you, locally and globally, and how it affects your plans, goals, and life decisions.

Even if "the world economy" feels too big to fit into your routine, there are three basic channels through which it hits your finances:

- **International trade and exchange rates** — when the U.S. dollar strengthens, imports become more expensive; parts, technology, and even some foods can rise in price, putting pressure on your cost of living.
- **Interest rates and monetary policy** — central banks adjust policy rates to fight inflation; higher rates make credit and financing more expensive and often slow consumption.

- **The business cycle and employment** — weak growth or recession usually means fewer hires, stagnant wages, and more insecurity in the job market.

When you understand these channels, headlines stop being alarms and start becoming intelligent warning signals.

No matter what country you live in, some economic phenomena tend to shape everyday life:

- Inflation, which erodes the value of your income and your savings.
- The central bank policy rate, which affects the cost of credit and the return on conservative investments.
- The exchange rate, which influences everything from your next phone to the price of goods that depend on imports.
- A fragile or informal job market, which makes many people more vulnerable to changes in the economic environment.

If you earn $3,000 per month and inflation averages 6% per year, then in 10 years what you buy today with $3,000 would cost about $5,373. In other words, if your income doesn't grow, your purchasing power is effectively cut almost in half.

Understanding this is not pessimism. It's preparation, and preparation is the tool that helps you stop suffering the economy and start using it in your favor.

The key is not just knowing concepts, but acting on them. Practical moves include:

- Keep part of your assets protected against inflation (for example, inflation-linked bonds, real assets, or well-chosen real estate).
- Avoid taking on high-interest debt when rates are rising.
- Maintain liquidity so you can respond quickly in unstable periods.
- Diversify your sources of income so you don't depend on one job or one sector.

When the economy tightens, the prepared people don't just survive; they spot opportunities. Prices adjust, assets fall, and those with cash flow and liquidity can buy quality at a discount.

You are not a hostage to the economy. But if you ignore it, it can catch you unprotected.

Inflation, Rates, and Exchange: t he Three Forces That Move Your Money

Inflation, interest rates, and exchange rates are three major forces that shape your financial life. Economics may look like complicated charts and technical speeches, but the effects are very concrete in your budget.

- **1) Inflation: the Silent Thief of Purchasing Power**

Inflation is a broad and sustained increase in prices. Milk, bread, and meat get more expensive—even when your salary doesn't rise, or rises too little.

What you planned to buy "later" can suddenly require much more money. And investments that earn "X% per year" can have a real return (after inflation) that is near zero, or negative.

People with income that doesn't adjust lose purchasing power. People who invest with a long-term view and diversify are more resilient.

How to reduce inflation's impact:

- Prioritize investments that can beat inflation (for example, inflation-linked bonds, real assets, and carefully selected real estate).
- Keep part of your portfolio liquid for emergencies, because inflationary periods can also create opportunities.
- Review spending regularly; some categories inflate faster (entertainment, travel, imported goods, electronics).

Buffett's "low tide" idea applies here: ignoring inflation eventually exposes you.

- **2) Interest Rates: the Price of Money**

Interest is the cost of money, and one of the engines of the economy. You've seen how rates impact financing, loans, and even the return on conservative investments.

When rates go up, borrowing becomes more expensive (mortgages, auto loans, personal credit). Consumption tends to slow, and companies often feel the pressure.

Higher rates can also make fixed-income investments more attractive. When rates are low, credit tends to be cheaper and risk assets may rise, while conservative yields shrink.

What does this mean in your life:

- If you carry variable-rate debt, rising rates can push your monthly payments higher.
- If you invest, higher rates can create good entry points, along with market volatility.
- If your plan ignores the possibility of high rates, you can get squeezed when installments rise.

How to protect yourself:

- Prioritize paying down or renegotiating high-interest debt: this destroys wealth faster than inflation.
- When financing, prefer fixed rates when possible to reduce surprises.
- Build a portfolio with a conservative core that benefits from higher rates, plus growth assets aligned with your time horizon.

- **3) Exchange Rates and Globalization: the International Reflection in Your Pocket**

The exchange rate, how much your currency is worth against the U.S. dollar and other currencies, can change your costs and your investment results.

- Electronics, travel abroad, and imported goods become more expensive when your currency weakens.
- Many local products also rise in price when they rely on imported inputs or global commodities priced in dollars.
- For investors, exporters or companies with foreign-currency revenue can benefit from a weaker local currency.

Why this matters for planning:

- If you plan to buy imported items, study abroad, or travel, consider that exchange rates can move the target upward.
- As an investor, geographic diversification and exposure to strong currencies can provide protection, not mandatory, but helpful.
- In countries with frequent currency swings, liquidity and reserves are even more important to absorb turbulence.

Once you understand inflation, rates, and exchange dynamics, economics stops being "for economists" and becomes a tool for better decisions: where to invest, when to borrow, and how to protect your plan.

Economic Scenarios: Make Your Plan Adaptive, Not Fragile

Because the world changes, your plan has to change too. In finance, it's as important to know that the economy moves as it is to know you can adjust to it.

Below are three illustrative scenarios. The goal isn't to predict the future: it's to prepare for it.

Scenario A: Optimistic
In this scenario:

- Inflation cools toward ~3% per year
- Interest rates fall toward ~8% per year
- The exchange rate stabilizes or improves modestly
- Employment strengthens and average income improves

How this can affect your finances:

- Financing and investing become more accessible
- Conservative yields shrink, pushing you to seek growth alternatives
- Consumption tends to rise, so the temptation to take on debt increases

Plan adjustments:

- Consider increasing contributions to medium/long-term investments
- It may be a good moment to evaluate financing for a home or business
- Even in good times, keep your emergency fund: optimism is not "no risk"

Scenario B: Moderate
A common "base case":

- Inflation around ~5%

- Rates around ~12% per year
- A volatile exchange rate
- Slow growth (~2–3%)

Impacts:

- Credit is expensive but still viable
- Conservative investments deliver reasonable returns
- Employment and income can fluctuate

Plan adjustments:

- Prioritize paying down high-rate debt and avoid new credit when possible
- Maintain or increase inflation protection in your portfolio
- Avoid committing more than ~30–40% of income to housing and credit
- Revisit medium-term goals—timelines may need to extend

Scenario C: Challenging

A stress scenario you should consider:

- Inflation above ~8% per year
- Very high rates (~15–20%+)
- A weak local currency against the dollar
- Zero or negative growth

Direct impacts:

- Financing becomes difficult or unattractive
- Conservative investments may still fail to beat inflation
- Imported goods and input costs jump
- Active income becomes less stable

Survival and strategy adjustments:

- Prioritize liquidity: build a stronger emergency fund
- Diversify income (active + passive) as much as possible
- Consider real assets and businesses that benefit from currency movements
- Cut variable spending with discipline and focus on what matters
- Delay major purchases and heavy financing if needed

Practical Exercise: Make the Economy Part of Your Plan

Now that you understand how inflation, rates, and exchange movements affect your finances, it turns understanding into action.

Grab a notebook, a spreadsheet, or your notes app and follow these steps:

Step 1 — Choose your "preferred" scenario and your "precaution" scenario

- Scenario A (Optimistic)
- Scenario B (Moderate)
- Scenario C (Challenging)

Mark which one seems most likely for your current life, and which one you will use as your contingency plan.

Step 2 — Stress-test your goals under the chosen scenario

For each financial goal (short, medium, long term), answer:

- Does this goal still make sense under this scenario?
- If inflation rises to 5%+ for a sustained period, is my plan still realistic?
- If rates rise to 15%+, can I keep my monthly contribution without breaking my budget?
- If the exchange rate spikes, will this goal become much more expensive than I planned?

Adjust as needed: longer timelines, different contributions, more conservative instruments, or a different path.

Step 3 — Adjust your investment plan

- **In Scenario A**: you can take slightly more risk, increase contributions, and diversify toward higher-return instruments.
- **In Scenario B**: keep balance: protect capital while pursuing moderate growth.
- **In Scenario C**: focus on liquidity, reserves, and risk reduction while positioning for opportunities when conditions improve.

Write down:

- "How much will I invest per month now?"
- "Which instruments will I prioritize (government bonds, CDs, money-market funds, REITs, etc.)?"

- "When will I review this plan?" (suggestion: every 3 months)

Step 4 — Define review triggers

So, your plan doesn't get forgotten, set triggers that force a review, for example:

- When the central bank policy rate moves more than ±2 percentage points
- When the USD exchange rate moves more than ±10% in six months
- When annual inflation prints above 7%
- Or simply a full review every 6–12 months

Put this on your calendar: your financial plan is a living system.

Step 5 — Your commitment statement

Write to yourself:

I take control of my financial life,
understanding that the economic environment affects me,
but it does not control me.
I prepare, adjust, and I prosper.
My financial plan does not depend on luck.
It depends on choices.
Sign and date it. Keep it somewhere visible.

Now, you have more than knowledge: you have a map to respond. The economy will move, and the people who are prepared are the ones who suffer less and benefit more.

Making money works for you isn't only about investing well. It's having strategy, systems, adaptabilityand acting with intent.

CHAPTER 17

Emergency fund: your shock absorber

This chapter is about real financial preparation and protection, about developing the awareness to shield yourself against the unexpected.

When Everything Fails, What Holds You Up?

Imagine jumping out of a plane without a parachute. Sounds absurd, right?

But that's exactly what most people do when they live with no emergency savings.

The problem isn't falling, everyone falls at some point. The problem is having nothing to soften the impact.

This chapter is urgent for anyone, at many stages of life, even for people who already understand finance. It's worth revisiting whenever a new situation arises.

Many readers reach this point wanting to organize, invest, and grow financially, and that's excellent. But no plan survives without a foundation.

An emergency fund is that foundation. It's the first layer of your financial security.

- It helps you breathe when you lose a job.
- It helps you keep your dignity during illness.
- It keeps you from going into debt when the car breaks down or the refrigerator dies.
- It prevents an unexpected event from turning into a financial tragedy.

I use the parachute image because it's simple and visual. A parachute doesn't prevent the fall, but it prevents the fall from destroying you.

- Yes, you can fall, but you land safely.
- Yes, you can make mistakes, but you have time to recover.
- Yes, you can stop working for a period, and still live with dignity.

And like a parachute, an emergency fund has to be built before the fall. After the plane is down, it's too late.

In practice, an emergency fund is a separate pool of money, typically 3 to 12 months of essential living costs, kept in a safe place with high liquidity.

It is not an investment to get rich. It is the cushion that protects you from life's unpredictability.

Ironically, many people rush into stocks, crypto, or sophisticated funds without first building this base. Then, when a real emergency hits, they are forced to sell at the worst time, accept losses, borrow, or panic.

Situations That Require an Emergency Fund

- Sudden loss or reduction of income (layoff, clients disappearing)
- Health problems that create unplanned expenses
- Medical expenses for you or someone close
- Accidents, theft, car repairs, or home repairs
- Family changes (divorce, a child's birth)
- Relocation or restarting life in another city

If you've never faced any of these, great. But it's usually only a matter of time. Life doesn't ask if you're ready: it just happens.

Real Examples

- Maria, 39, nursing assistant: lost her job during the pandemic. It took 5 months to find a new role. Her emergency fund kept her afloat without high-interest debt.
- Rafael, 27, self-employed: had a motorcycle accident and couldn't work for 3 months. A disciplined emergency fund protected his bills and his mental health.

- João, 53, manager: never built a fund. After 20 years at the same company, he was laid off. He relied on credit cards and loans, and the stress multiplied.

All three went through something hard. Only two had a parachute.

An emergency fund isn't a luxury: it's a shield. Like a seatbelt, you don't wear it hoping for a crash. You wear it because you understand reality. Start now. Even with little. Even without knowing everything. The peace it brings is worth more than any quick profit.

How to Build It (Even on a Tight Income)

Now that you understand why the emergency fund matters, the next question is: how do you build it in practice, especially when money feels tight?

The good news: this is absolutely doable, even for people who feel like they barely make it to the end of the month.

A common guideline is:

- If your income is stable (salary): save 3 to 6 months of essential expenses.
- If your income varies (self-employed, freelancers, business owners): save 6 to 12 months.

Important: the target is based on your essential monthly expenses, not on your income.

Example Calculation

Imagine your essential monthly costs are:

- Rent: $1,200
- Food: $1,000
- Basic bills: $600
- Transportation: $400
- Health insurance: $300
- Total: $3,500

If you have a stable salary, a 6-month fund would be about $21,000.

If your income varies, a 12-month fund would be about $42,000.

"Does that feel like a lot?" It can be intimidating at first. But the goal is not to save it all at once. The goal is to build it month by month, like a commitment to your freedom.

A Simple 4-Step Plan

- Define a small monthly starting amount. Even $50, $100, or $200—the key is to take the first step.
- Open a separate, easy-access account with reasonable yield. A high-yield savings account, a money-market fund, or short-term government instruments can work—avoid anything that takes days to access or swings in value.
- Automate deposits. If you can schedule the transfer right after payday, it is even better. This prevents the "spend first, save later" pattern. Pay yourself first.
- Set milestone goals. Instead of focusing only on $21,000, celebrate progress: your first $1,000; then half the fund; then the full amount.

Each milestone is a real victory on the path to peace of mind.

Make It a Mental Commitment

It's not just an account: it's an internal decision. It's when you look at your life and say:

I respect myself enough to prepare for the unexpected.

I prefer the calm of security over the anxiety of uncertainty.

I choose to sleep well, even if everything goes sideways.

That mindset changes the game. It creates stability, and stability improves decisions.

What NOT to Do With Your Emergency Fund

- Don't invest it in volatile assets. Stocks, crypto, or REITs may belong in your growth plan, but not in your emergency base.
- Don't let it sit earning nothing. Avoid leaving it idle. Keep it liquid, safe, and earn a reasonable return.

- Don't use it for non-emergencies. It is not for a new phone, a trip, or a Black Friday "deal." It is your emotional and financial seatbelt.

Even some "emergencies" should be handled without draining the fund entirely. For example, if your car is beyond repair and you need a replacement, plan so you don't wipe out your protection.

Track It

Create a simple sheet or note with:

- Target emergency fund amount
- Current balance
- Next monthly contribution
- Estimated timeline to completion

Update it monthly and celebrate progress: responsibly. Progress you can see is progress you can sustain.

You don't need to be rich to build an emergency fund. You need discipline, patience, and awareness.

And by starting today, whether with $50, $100, or whatever is possible, you're already far ahead of the person who keeps postponing it.

The Emotional Power of an Emergency Fund

Money saved changes how you think, feel, decide—and sleep. Literally. An emergency fund is not just a bank balance; it's an emotional shield. *"Have you ever felt that stomach drop when an unexpected bill arrives? " Or the tight chest when the car needs a $2,000 repair?" "Or the knot in your throat when you hear about layoffs?"*

With an emergency fund, the surprise still exists, but it doesn't panic. You breathe. You think. You evaluate. You decide.

Instead of reacting in desperation, you respond with clarity, and that difference changes everything.

Financial stress is widely associated with anxiety, depressive symptoms, insomnia, family conflict, and chronic stress. An emergency fund doesn't remove hardship, but it reduces fear.

- You feel less trapped in a toxic job or relationship.
- You can say "no" to bad offers with more clarity.
- You avoid impulsive financial decisions.

- You reduce self-sabotage driven by desperation.

Freedom Isn't Luxury—It's the Result of Preparation

You've heard people say:

- *"I'm only staying in this job because I can't afford to stop."*
- *"I'd love to move, but if I do it now, I won't make it."*
- *"My dream is to start a business, but I'm afraid I won't pay the bills."*

All of that comes from the same place: no foundation. The emergency fund builds the foundation. With it, you build real choices—not just survival.

The freedom to pause for a month. To say, "not now." To think calmly. That's worth more than a vacation paid for in ten installments.

The Reserve Protects You From Emotional Blackmail

In many personal, family, and even professional relationships, money becomes a form of leverage. People without reserves tolerate situations they didn't choose—because they have no runway.

Those with an emergency fund have options. And options are a form of power.

Don't Touch the Parachute Before the Fall

Building an emergency fund takes discipline. Protecting it takes even more, because once the balance grows, temptation grows too.

The first trap is self-justification. You tell yourself:

- *"I worked so hard this month—I deserve this."*
- *"This deal ends tomorrow..."*
- *"It's not an emergency, but it's a unique opportunity."*
- *"I'll replace it later."*
- *"It's just a little..."*

Those phrases are common, and dangerous. They make a detour feel reasonable. And once you break the rule, it becomes easier to break it again.

An emergency fund is not for comfort. It's for safety. If you can avoid the expense, avoid it.

Another trap is emotional spending. A hard day, anxiety, stress, then you buy something as a reward. Self-care is real, but it should not be funded by your protection.

If you want a "treat," plan for it: create a separate "fun fund," but don't touch the parachute.

A third trap is using your shield to rescue others.

- A friend asks for a loan "just until next month."
- A relative is in trouble.
- Someone wants to start a business and asks for "trust money."

Helping can be noble. But if you compromise your emergency fund, you become the next person who needs help.

Don't help others with the money that protects you. Help with time, listening, and guidance. If you truly have surplus, then you can help financially—without risking your foundation.

Helping out of guilt can become emotional debt—and the damage is doubled.

Another trap is mixing the emergency fund with your everyday account. If your reserve sits where you receive income and pay bills, it's easy to lose track and "accidentally" spend it.

A better solution is a separate account or separate instrument—clearly labeled EMERGENCY FUND. That creates psychological distance: it stops feeling like "available balance" and becomes "last line of defense."

The final trap is chasing yield. You hear that savings accounts pay little, so you place your reserve in riskier assets. Then an emergency comes, and your balance is down when you need it most.

The emergency fund is not about maximizing returns. It's about protection and liquidity. It's better to earn less and stay safe than to reach for more and be exposed when you need it most.

How to Protect Your Fund

- Name the money. Label it EMERGENCY FUND everywhere—account name, spreadsheet, notes. This reinforces the commitment.
- Create personal rules. Example: "I only use it if I lose income or face a true medical emergency."
- Build parallel goals. A separate account for fun, another for travel, another for dreams—so you don't raid the reserve.
- Review monthly. Staying connected to the purpose protects discipline.
- Use accountability. Share your rules with a trusted person (spouse, mentor) to strengthen self-control.

Having funds is an act of self-respect. Protecting funds is an act of maturity. Your future self will thank you.

Reflection

Ask yourself:

- *"How many months could I live today without income—while maintaining dignity and calm?"*
- *"What can I do to improve that starting now?"*

And if you've already started building this foundation: how many "months of peace" have you already built?

Do the Math Today

Grab paper and pen, or open your notes app.

- List your essential monthly expenses (housing, basic food, fixed bills, transportation, health, education if applicable, and other indispensable commitments).
- Add them up and write your minimum monthly cost of living with dignity.
- Calculate your emergency fund targets: minimum (3 months), ideal (6 months), advanced (12 months).
- Write how much you currently have saved as a real emergency fund (separate, liquid, available).
- Calculate how many months you are protected today.

Example: if you have $4,800 saved and spend $3,200/month, your reserve covers about 1.5 months.

Now: What's Your Plan?

Write:

- *"How much can I save per month, realistically?"*
- *"What is my target for the next 3 months?"*
- *"What is my goal by the end of this year?"*

Make the plan visible. People who see the path are more likely to follow it. The question that changes everything is: "How many months of peace do I have today?" And even more: "How many months of peace do I want—and am I willing to build?"

Commitment

Close your eyes for a moment. Imagine a hard season: unemployment, illness, divorce, an accident, a loss. Now imagine facing it with a safety reserve. "Which version of that story do you want to live?"

Write and repeat:

Today I begin, or continue, building my financial peace.
I am responsible for myself.
I deserve calm.
I don't wait for the problem to arrive.
I prepare.
My emergency fund is my vote of respect for my life.

The best time to build a shelter is before the storm.
— American proverb

Money is like oxygen in a crisis: you only notice it when it runs out. The peace of someone who prepared is worth more than any quick win. You may not control the world, but you can control your parachute.

An emergency fund is the quiet pillar that supports higher flights. Without it, any turbulence becomes free fall. With it, even a fall becomes a softer landing.

Start where you are, with what you hav, but start.

CHAPTER 18

The psychology of money

People say money starts in your head, not in your wallet. "Have you ever wondered why two people with the same paycheck can live with completely different financial realities?"

"Or why, even earning more, do some people stay in debt, anxious, and without any savings?"

The answer is rarely in the spreadsheet.

It is in the mind. Money is far more emotional than rational. We don't make financial decisions with a calculator. We make them with our heart.

With fear.

With guilt.

With need.

With impulse.

With what we heard as children.

With what we lived through in the past.

Money is an extension of our psychology.

That is why knowing how to invest doesn't help if you emotionally sabotage yourself.

It all starts in childhood. Think for a moment:

- *"What did your parents tell you about money?"*
- *"What was the atmosphere at home when the topic was bills, salary, debt?"*
- *"Did you hear more phrases like "that's not for people like us" or "money doesn't grow on trees"?"*
- *"Did you watch your parents fight because of money?"*

Those experiences form our unconscious beliefs.

They stay with us, even when we forget them.

If you grew up hearing that "money is dirty," you may unconsciously avoid having much.

If you learned that "people who get rich are dishonest," you may sabotage legitimate opportunities.

The cycle of financial self-sabotage often begins when money is treated as something illegitimate - as an excuse for why we don't have it in our lives.

- Many people earn well - but spend it all.
- Others manage to save - but never invest.
- Some grow - and then lose everything.

That happens because what determines your financial situation isn't only how much you earn, but what you believe you deserve and can sustain.

Some people, deep down, believe:

- *"I'm not good enough to have a lot."*
- *"If I get rich, people will ask me for money."*
- *"Rich people end up alone."*
- *"Money will make me a worse person."*
- *"With money, I'll lose who I am."*

Without realizing it, you build internal barriers to prosperity. I'm not talking about anything supernatural or mystical. I'm simply showing you how emotions can take over your wallet.

Each emotion distorts how we relate to money:

- Fear: freezes investing, paralyzes decisions, makes you hoard without purpose.
- Anxiety: pushes impulsive spending to compensate for an inner emptiness.
- Guilt: makes you give money to everyone, even at your own expense.
- Anger: can trigger drastic and destructive choices ("if I can't make it, I'll blow it all").
- Neediness: looks for love in consumption.
- The card becomes a crutch.

- Credit becomes comfortable.
- The statement becomes punishment.

The psychological profile of your wallet

Have you ever stopped observing yourself? See which of these profiles feels closest to you:

- **The Anxious Saver** - saves compulsively but never feels safe.
- **The Emotional Spender** - buys to fill voids and regrets it later.
- **The Financial Rescuer** - keeps saving others but doesn't take care of themself.
- **The Unprepared Optimist** - believes everything will work out, even without a plan.
- **The Rigid Controller** - has everything in a spreadsheet but struggles to actually live.
- **The Financial Avoider** - avoids checking accounts, delays decisions, ignores debts.

We all carry traits of these profiles.
The key is to recognize them and bring them into balance.

The psychology of money is the invisible foundation of your financial reality.

It doesn't help to change jobs, start a business, or invest well if the same beliefs that keep you stuck are still living inside you.

It is time to look inward.

Because your wallet only truly changes when your mind changes first. We need to learn how to reprogram those beliefs and build a clean prosperity mindset, conscious and free of guilt.

Yes, money can and should be your ally. If your financial decisions reflect your emotions, memories, and beliefs, then one powerful truth follows:

- You can change this story.
- You can reprogram your relationship with money.

And it doesn't matter your age, your background, your education, or your past.

What matters is what you're willing to do from now on.

- Limiting beliefs and how to rewrite them

- Limiting beliefs are absorbed as "absolute truths." But many of them are not yours. They were inherited. Repeated. Imposed. Never questioned.

Phrases like:

- *"Money doesn't buy happiness."*
- *"If you're born poor, you die poor."*
- *"People with a lot of money are greedy."*
- *"It's wrong to want to get rich."*
- *"That's not for people like us."*
- *"Money disappears fast anyway..."*

These ideas, repeatedly since childhood, have become mental filters. And over time you start acting to confirm those "truths" - without even noticing.

The good news is that any belief can be rewritten. But like any re-education, it takes awareness, practice, and time.

First action: identify your inner phrases.

Grab a piece of paper. Write down the first sentence that comes to mind when you think about:

- Wealth
- Rich people
- Having a lot of money
- Spending on yourself
- Running out of money
- Charging for your work
- Investing bigger

Don't filter. Be honest.
You'll be surprised by what comes out.
Those sentences reveal how your mind is programmed.

Second action: confront them with reality.

Now, for each limiting sentence, write a more realistic and healthier counterstatement.

Examples:

"Money doesn't buy happiness."

- -> ***"Money doesn't buy happiness, but it can buy safety, time, and opportunities that help me live happier."***

"People with a lot of money are greedy."

- -> ***"There are good and bad people in every social class. Money reveals; it doesn't transform."***

"If you're born poor, you die poor."

- -> ***"I know stories of people who changed their reality through effort, study, and good decisions."***

Replace judgment with curiosity. Replace fear with awareness. Replace scarcity with construction.

Now rewrite your financial narrative and repeat to yourself phrases like:

- *"I deserve to live with financial peace."*
- *"Having money allows me to take better care of myself and the people I love."*
- *"I can grow without guilt."*
- *"Prosperity is natural when there is awareness."*
- *"I trust myself to manage more - and manage it better."*
- *"Money is my ally - not my enemy."*

Don't underestimate this exercise.
Repetition creates a new internal pattern.
And an internal pattern creates different external behavior.

From new beliefs to new behavior

Changing what you think isn't magic, but it changes what you do. And action starts small - while transformation is huge. Take one step at a time, from trauma to ownership.

If you've suffered with money - humiliation, debt, bankruptcy, lack - it's natural to feel fear, resistance, or even shame. But your past doesn't have to be your destination. Your history explains to you, but it doesn't define who you can become. Step by step, you can move from guilt and paralysis to conscious leadership of your financial life.

You don't need to become someone else to change your relationship with money.

You need to become the best version of yourself: more awake, more aware, freer.

The change starts in the mind but transforms the wallet.

It is essential to understand how everyday emotions - joy, sadness, anger, neediness - shape every purchase we make, and how we can take back control of that emotional process. Develop self-awareness so you can decide with more balance and clarity.

When your emotions are about to decide for you, pause and think about your last unplanned purchase.

Maybe delivery on a stressful day. Or a new piece of clothing to feel better. Or an oversized gift for someone - just to please.

Now ask yourself: "what was I feeling at that moment?"

The answer is almost always in the emotions. The card went through, but the decision was made by the heart.

The neuroscience behind emotional spending

The human brain has two systems:

- The Rational System (neocortex), which analyzes, compares, and decides logically.
- The Emotional System (limbic system), which reacts through impulse, fear, pleasure, and pain.

Most of the time, the emotional system takes the lead.
Especially when we are:

- Tired
- Sad
- Euphoric
- Anxious
- Frustrated
- Needy

In other words: when we're most vulnerable, we're most susceptible to bad money decisions.

Let's see how each emotion can distort your relationship with money and its financial impact:

1. Sadness
- Tends to increase the search for immediate pleasure.
- Example: "I'm sad, so I deserve something good right now."
- Result: spending on food, online shopping, "treats."

2. Anger
- Creates impulsivity and a desire to compensate.
- Example: "Since they made me mad, I'll do what I want!"
- Result: drastic decisions, bad investments, "financial revenge."

3. Neediness
- Leads to spending to be accepted or recognized.
- Example: "I need to impress, please, show my value."
- Result: excessive gifts, brand-name clothes, living above your budget.

4. Anxiety
- Anticipates rewards.
- Example: "I don't know what tomorrow brings, so I'll enjoy today."

- Result: installment purchases, no emergency fund, disorganization.

5. Euphoria

- Creates a false sense of invincibility.
- Example: "Now everything will work out! I can spend."
- Result: expansion without planning, promises bigger than reality.

All of these emotions are human. But if you don't recognize them, they begin to control your wallet.

Self-observation: questions that create freedom

Before each decision, start asking yourself:

- *"What am I feeling right now?"*
- *"Is this purchase a need or an emotion?"*
- *"If I wait 24 hours, will I still want this?"*
- *"Am I trying to fill a void that money can't fix?"*

Questions create awareness.
Awareness creates clarity.
Clarity generates freedom.

Five practical strategies to handle emotions and money

- **The 24-hour rule:**

About making an unplanned purchase? Wait one day.
If it still makes sense, reassess calmly.

- **Create an "Emotional Money Journal":**

Write down impulse purchases and what you were feeling at the time.
After a month, the patterns will jump out.

- **Build a "Relief Fund":**

A small reserve ($100, $200) just to ease emotional moments - without damaging your budget.

- **Practice conscious buying:**

Ask: does this bring me closer to my goals?
Does this represent who I want to be?

- **Use time in your favor:**

Most emotions pass.

- Waiting 15 minutes can change your impulse.
- Waiting one day can transform your perspective.

Your inner dialogue and a new narrative

Talk to yourself like your best friend would:

- "I know today was hard, but sabotaging myself won't help."
- "I deserve something good - but within what truly does me good."
- "Today is one day. My life is worth more than one moment."
- "I don't need to prove anything to anyone with my money."

This kind of self-talk reprograms your emotional response.

You start to feel pride - not regret - after each choice.

The money you lose to impulse is smaller than the power you lose over yourself. But that can change, if you start listening to yourself, and respecting your emotions without letting them drive your financial life.

Family, culture, and society: the voices in your head

Family, cultural, and social beliefs quietly shape our money behavior. Identifying, understanding, and transforming those influences is a key step to mastering the voices inside your head.

You think you make financial decisions alone, but in reality many voices speak inside you.

Childhood voices. Parents' voices. Society's voice. Social media's voice. An entire culture. And until you recognize these influences, they will keep deciding for you.

The invisible inheritance from parents and caregivers - even when they never taught you finance directly - is often the main culprit behind money imbalance. Silence teaches too.

Think:

- *"Were your parents afraid to talk about money?"*
- *"Did the mood change around bill-paying time?"*
- *"When money came in, did they celebrate it or hide it?"*
- *"Was there abundance, scarcity, showing off, excessive control?"*

Those behaviors plant seeds:

- People raised in scarcity may become hoarders or compulsive spenders.
- People who watched fights about money may develop a phobia of bills.
- People who were deprived may become indulgent.
- People who were spoiled may never learn to plan.

"It's not about what you were taught - it's about what you absorbed without noticing." And that inheritance is not a sentence. Many people learn from those patterns and build the opposite - breaking paradigms and constructing a financial life worthy of specialists. The seed may come from family, but we still have to overcome adversity throughout life.

Beyond family, cultural and social-class beliefs also leave their marks. Phrases like:

- *"Money changes people."*
- *"So-and-so got arrogant after getting rich."*
- *"The rich humiliate; the poor have good hearts."*
- *"Anyone who works too much is exploited; anyone who earns too much is suspicious."*

These sentences create a culture of guilt around prosperity, as if growing financially meant betraying your roots.

Result: many people grow up ashamed of prospering.

They begin to hide. To downplay. To lose opportunities out of fear of judgment.

Social media pressure and comparison

Social media completes the picture. This new layer of influence is even more powerful because it is designed - via algorithms - to distract, manipulate, and induce actions that often lead to unnecessary spending and losses, directly impacting your financial education and management.

You open Instagram and see:

- Cars you don't have
- Homes you can't afford
- Clothes that aren't your reality
- Unreachable (or staged) lifestyles

And then, without noticing, the thoughts appear:

- *"I'm behind."*
- *"Everyone has it, except me."*
- *"I need to show something too."*
- *"If I can't keep up, I'm failing."*

But what you see is the prettiest slice of someone else's chaos.

Comparing your backstage to other people's stage is the formula for frustration.

Silent family expectations

No few challenges are silent family expectations.

Many people grow up with invisible burdens:

- Being the provider
- Supporting parents or siblings
- Fulfilling the dream their parents couldn't
- Maintaining the family lifestyle, even without the means
- Being successful "to make everyone proud"

These pressures create:

- Guilt for saying no

- Shame for asking for help
- Fear of making a financial mistake
- Commitments bigger than your income

And then people go into debt not because they're irresponsible, but because of emotional obligation. You need to identify what is yours and what was imposed.

Try this exercise:

- Write your view on: earning, spending, investing, helping, saving, showing off.
- Ask: is this what I truly believe, or what I was told was right?
- Evaluate: does this belief bring me closer to the life I want, or does it push me away from it?

Every belief must pass a useful test.
If it no longer serves you, it must be reframed.
Often the change begins by rewriting the family narrative.
You can honor your roots without repeating the patterns. Internalize phrases like:

- "My parents did the best they could - and now I can do different."
- "I can love my family without carrying their money fears."
- "Growing financially doesn't make me less humble."
- "I don't need to sabotage myself to keep bonds - I can build new paths."
- "I don't need to prove anything to anyone except myself."

You are not a traitor for prospering. You are a bridge to evolution.

The psychology of money is about recognizing where your ideas came from.

"Who laid the bricks of your financial thinking?"
"And which ones will you keep - or replace - from now on?"

Asking for help - with dignity

You must learn how to seek emotional or financial help with dignity, awareness, and lightness.

Because no one grows alone. Asking for help is a sign of strength, not failure.

"How many times have you pretended everything was fine financially - when inside you were to your limit?"

"How many times did you want to ask for help, but pride, fear of judgment, or shame were stronger?"

We grow up hearing money is private.
That "you don't talk about amounts."
That "if you handle it, you handle it."
But the truth is everyone needs help at some point.
Especially with money, which involves numbers and emotions at the same time.

Isolation is an invisible enemy. Most people with financial problems:

- Feel ashamed to talk
- Hide it from friends and family
- Keep up appearances
- Keep "kicking the can down the road"
- Suffering in silence

Silence turns difficulty into guilt.
Guilt paralyzes.
Paralyzed, the problem grows.
And the cycle repeats.
"If I had spoken sooner..." is a phrase we hear often from people who broke down.

Signs it's time to ask for help

- You feel anxious just thinking about opening your bank app.
- You do mental math every month to see if you'll have enough.
- You avoid answering the phone because you're afraid of collections.
- You can't save even $50 per month.
- You feel ashamed to say you have no money.
- You've thought about "solving it" with expensive loans.

If you identify with two or more of these, it is time to ask for help - before it becomes a deeper hole.

This book is certainly helping you, and every time you reread it, it will help even more. But sometimes we need external support, such as:

1. Financial advisors

Professionals specialized in personal and family financial planning who can help you:

- Organize debts
- Build a realistic budget
- Create an emergency fund and investment plan
- Set viable goals

2. Financial therapy

When the issue isn't only technical but emotional.

For those who struggle with:

- Guilt around spending or saving
- Toxic family dynamics tied to money
- Self-sabotage when things start going well
- Fear of prospering
- Chronic anxiety because of debt

A therapist helps untie invisible knots that sabotage your prosperity.

3. Mentors or trustworthy friends

Not always a specialist is needed.

Sometimes a more experienced friend, a balanced relative,

someone you respect can be the first support to bring clarity and help map a plan.

Asking for help is courage, not weakness

Imagine a boat with a leak.

You can keep trying to plug the hole with your hands.

But if you don't ask for help, the water will rise and eventually you'll sink.

Asking for help is throwing away a life preserver.

It's getting air.

It's giving you the right to breathe again.

You don't need to have all the answers.

You only need to take the first step.

That first step is often the biggest challenge, so here is how to start the conversation. Find a person - a friend, a family member, or a professional - take off the armor, and say:

"Hey, I'm going through a delicate financial moment.

It's not easy to talk about this, but I admire your balance and I wanted to see if we could talk.

I'm not asking for money - just clarity and maybe some direction."

Or:

"I've been trying to organize my financial life, but I feel stuck.

Do you know someone trustworthy who could guide me seriously?"

Be clear. Be honest. Be humble.

When you're real, you usually find open doors.

The biggest financial mistake isn't making a mistake.

It's not asking for help while there's still time.

Don't isolate. Don't be ashamed.

You're human - and humans need each other.

A healthy, lasting relationship with money

"How do you turn your relationship with money into something healthy, lasting, and liberating - not imprisoning?"

You may have arrived here with fear, doubts, trauma, or regret. But what matters now is the path you choose to walk.

Your relationship with money doesn't need to be a battlefield.

It can, and should , be a partnership of growth, balance, and peace.

Money isn't the villain of your story

Many people grew up believing money was a problem.
Others believed it was the magic solution to everything.
Both extremes are wrong.

- Money is neither villain nor savior.
- Money is a tool.
- Money is a mirror.
- Money is a language - of your self-esteem, your boundaries, your decisions.

And like any powerful tool, it depends on who is using it.
Healing your relationship with money is a process, and it happens in stages:

- **Awareness**: noticing there's something wrong - a repeating pattern, an unhealed pain.
- **Acceptance:** stopping the self-blame and looking at your journey with compassion.
- **Action:** seeking information, help, practices, and new habits.
- **Persistence**: continuing even when it feels hard, strange, or slow.
- **Transformation**: when the new pattern settles and becomes a lifestyle.

It's like re-educating your palate.
At first it feels like something is missing.
Then you feel free from dependence.

And finally, you choose consciously, and enjoy the lightness.

A healthy relationship with money means:

- Knowing exactly how much you earn and spend, without fear of looking.
- Having clear priorities.
- Being able to say "yes" with joy and "no" with confidence.
- Feeling proud to save and invest.
- Spending with purpose, not guilt.
- Feeling money is working for you, not against you.

A good relationship with money isn't having a lot.
It's having emotional mastery over what you already have - and building, step by step, what you want to reach.

I want to share special phrases for you to carry for life:

- *"Whoever doesn't master emotions doesn't master their money."*
- *"You are stronger than your last debt."*
- *"The bank balance can change. But your mind needs to change first."*
- *"Growing with lightness is possible."*
- *"Peace with money is more powerful than having millions with no direction."*
- *"You deserve to live calmly - without fear of the bill."*

The psychology of money isn't a mystery.
It's a journey of rediscovery.
Of re-education.
Of courage.
And of reconciliation.
Because money is part of your life.
And like everything that matters, it deserves attention, awareness, and care.
Be light. Be steady.
And keep moving forward - head up and wallet at peace.

CHAPTER 19

Small decisions, big destinies

Everyday decisions quietly shape your financial future, and small habits, repeated over time, can lead to meaningful change. But the real power comes from consistency and where you direct your money.

"Do you know that coffee is at the bakery?"

"Or that monthly subscription you don't even use anymore?"

"Or the temptation to order delivery on a random Wednesday, even though you have food at home?"

It may sound exaggerated to say these small decisions shape your financial destiny.

But the truth is: they do.

And not only your financial destiny - but they also shape your mindset, your discipline, and your future.

Financial success, most of the time, doesn't come from one big event, but from the sum of small daily choices.

The daily-coffee effect is invisible math, but let's do a simple calculation:

- One coffee a day: $8
- Five days a week: $40
- In one month: $160
- In one year: $1,920

If instead of spending that amount you invested the same $160 per month in a basic investment earning 0.6% per month (just as an illustration), in 20 years you would have more than $75,000. Yes - seventy-five thousand in coffee.

And think how many other small decisions you repeat without noticing. Please don't stop enjoying your wonderful coffee because of this. The secret is to identify the small "unnecessary" things - or expenses you didn't even realize you were paying - and understand that controlling the small leaks is what allows you to keep your pleasures with peace for the rest of your life.

The power of silent repetition

Every repeated action becomes a habit.

And habits become destiny.

You don't end up in debt because of one purchase, but because of the accumulation of small excesses.

Just like you won't become wealthy because of one good month, but because of repeating discipline.

Or, as the famous quote attributed to Aristotle says: ***"We are what we repeatedly do. Excellence, then, is not an act, but a habit."***

The same is true for disorganization: that's where the small decisions live that drain your money and you don't even notice.

Here are some choices that look innocent, but added up overtime, pushing you away from financial peace:

- Streaming subscriptions, apps, and clubs you don't use
- "Cheap" clothes that pile up and never get worn
- Eating out every day without control
- Bank fees that could be avoided
- Impulse buys at the grocery store
- Parties and dinners you pay for just to please others

None of these things are wrong by itself.

The problem is unconscious repetition with no purpose.

Awareness is the first step to change the game

You don't need to stop living, cut everything, or become a

financial monk. But you do need to start watching. Really looking at where your money is going.

Try this for one week: write down every expense, no matter how small. At the end, group them by type: food, transportation, entertainment, impulse buys, etc.

See how much you spent on "unplanned" or "unnecessary" items. This simple exercise will show you where the invisible leaks are. And more than that, it will show you what you're choosing to repeat.

Consistence is your new best friend

Most people's biggest difficulty with money isn't knowing what to do. It's sticking with what they started.

You've probably tried:

- Starting to save
- Downloading a finance app
- Tracking expenses
- Studying investing
- Cutting credit cards
- Stopping impulse buying

And then, after a few days or weeks, you went back to the old pattern. That didn't happen because you lack ability. It happened because you lacked consistency.

Consistency is built with small, sustainable decisions, made every day.

Think of a staircase with 100 steps.
You don't need to sprint it up.
You don't need to jump three at a time.
You don't need to reach the top right now.
You just need to climb one step per day.

One dollar saved.
One subscription canceled.
One meal cooked at home.

One bill reviewed calmly.
One budget conversation with someone you love.
One mistake corrected - without guilt.

It all seems small. But when it adds up, it transforms your life. You don't change your financial life with one mega-decision.

You change it with hundreds of conscious micro-decisions, made with intention and persistence.

The secret isn't in the extraordinary.

It's in the ordinary done with attention.

The avalanche effect of good decisions

A small positive habit can create a wave of change across your financial, emotional, physical, and even spiritual life.

"Have you noticed how one small decision can trigger a chain of unexpected events?"

Think about it:

- You wake up and make your bed.
- That sense of accomplishment motivates you to make a good breakfast.
- That breakfast gives you energy to leave on time.
- You get to work earlier, and that earns a compliment from your boss.
- The compliment motivates you to finish a pending report.
- At the end of the day, you feel so productive that you decide not to order delivery - and you cook something light at home.
- And when you go to sleep, you feel like you had a great day - all because you decided to make the bed.

That's the avalanche (or domino) effect.

One small action creates a chain of change across multiple areas of life. In the financial world, it can be even more visible: one good money decision tends to influence the rest.

Example:
You decide to cancel a $49.90 subscription you don't use.
With that money, you make a more rational grocery purchase.
You feel proud.
You decide to write that down in your finance notebook.
Then you review your bank statement for the week.
You find two more useless expenses.
You save $120.
With that, you start your first emergency fund.
For the first time, you feel in control.

The initial decision looked irrelevant. ut it activated a process of clarity, motivation, and empowerment.

Your brain seeks coherence

Our brain tries to stay consistent with our actions.

- If you start the day saving, you're more inclined to keep saving.
- If you start the month paying bills on time, you avoid chaos mid-month.
- If you start the week eating at home, you resist spending temptations more easily.

This is called cognitive consistency.
And it's a powerful ally for your financial health.
But be careful: the opposite is also true, and dangerous.
The avalanche effect works on the negative side too.
You ignore a small bill.
You think $80 won't make a difference.
You spend another $30 on something unnecessary.
By the end of the week, it adds up to $400 in waste.
You go into overdrafts to cover it.
Next month, you pay interest.
And a snowball forms that feels impossible to stop.

That's why the first wrong decision is the most dangerous one. Because it gives you internal permission to mess up again.

The 7-day challenge

Here is a powerful and simple plan: a practical challenge. For 7 days, make one small positive financial decision per day.

Examples:

- Don't buy something you normally buy without thinking
- Cancel one useless expense
- Track all your spending for the day
- Eat at home instead of going out
- Save $10
- Avoid an emotional trigger (like browsing shopping apps)
- Make a small sale (something sitting around that can become cash)
-

At the end of the week, observe:

- *"How do you feel?"*
- *"How much did you save?"*
- *"What other areas of your life have improved?"*

I guarantee you'll be surprised. Small wins strengthen identity. Each small right choice reinforces your identity as a disciplined person. Over time, your mind stops saying "I'm disorganized with money" and starts saying:

-
- *"I'm learning."*
- *"I'm in control."*
- *"I can improve."*
- *"I make good choices."*
- *"I'm in charge of my financial life."*

When identity changes, behavior follows naturally.

Don't underestimate the power of one small choice.
It can be the first brick of the house you dream of building.
The first step of the emergency fund will make you feel safe.
The first win that changes how you see yourself.
Small choices in the present can help you gain - or lose - decades in the future. Time becomes your greatest ally if you decide to start today, or your greatest enemy if you decide to neglect your financial life.

Imagine that today you decide to save $200 per month.
It may seem like little. Almost nothing.
Less than one pizza a week with soda.
You may think, "This won't change my life."
But if you invested that amount for 20 years at an average return of 0.6% per month (again, as an illustration), you would have more than $96,000.
Now reflect: "What if you had started five years ago?"
If you treat time as your most valuable resource, you will regret it and avoid wasting it. We can recover money; we can't recover time. Every time you postpone a smart decision, you lose years that could have been working in your favor.

People who understand this early can:

- Stop renting before 35
- Have a comfortable retirement by 55
- Pay for their kids' college without debt
- Work for pleasure - not desperation
- Have reserves for illness, crises, and surprises

It's not magic.
It's decision + time.
But this simple equation doesn't work for those who keep waiting "until there's extra."
Many people say:
"When I earn more, I'll start saving."
"When I have leftover money, I'll invest."
"When I finish paying this, then I'll organize everything."

The problem is: there is rarely leftover.
And the longer you wait, the harder it gets.
Here is a real example of the math of time:

- Person A starts investing $300 per month at age 25.

They do it for 10 years and then stop.

- Person B starts at age 35, also at $300 per month.

They invest until age 65.

Result: Person A, even after stopping, ends up with more accumulated money.

Why? Because time multiplies.

The earlier you plant, the bigger the harvest.
A seed ignored never becomes a tree.
It's not about saving thousands per month.
It's not about despising the first $50, $100, $150.

Those seeds, planted with good strategy and patience, become roots. And roots become trees. And trees protect you from storms.

Prosperity vs. putting out fires

You've probably seen:

- People with high income who live in debt
- Simple people who have properties, investments, peace
- Couples who live on the edge despite two good salaries
- Retirees who are calm even though they never earned much

The difference isn't how much someone earns.
It's what they repeat.
It's how much they respect time.
It's what they plant with intention.

Here's another real case with fictional names.
I call it "Dona Neide and the simple salon."

Dona Neide was a hairdresser in the suburbs. She never earned more than two minimum wages. But every month, at the end of her shift, she set aside $100 and saved it.

When new investment options appeared, she moved it into something simple but more profitable.

She did that for 25 years.

She never stopped living, traveling by bus, helping her children. But she didn't spend on impulse. She didn't live to "look rich."

When she turned 60, she had a paid-off home, solid savings, and a peace many executives never have. It all started with one simple decision repeated with respect for time.

Big achievements are made of small seeds planted with patience. Time is your greatest partner - as long as you decide to act in your favor, today.

Social pressure and comparison

Now let's talk about social pressure - something all of us face at different moments of life.

Comparison can pull you off focus. You need to cultivate your own path without falling into those social traps.

The desire to keep up with other people's spending patterns can distort solid plans.

To build an independent and healthy financial mindset, you need focus, understanding, and goals.

If you've ever felt embarrassed to have a simpler car, hesitated to decline an expensive invitation so you wouldn't seem "cheap," or bought something you didn't even want that much just because everyone else was buying it - you're not alone. That's 99% of people.

Comparison is one of the subtlest and most dangerous poisons for financial health.

The need to keep up turns good decisions into bad choices. And comparing yourself to someone else's life is the fastest shortcut to imbalance.

We live in a society that rewards appearances. Social media intensified it. Online, everyone looks well-dressed, traveling, eating out, buying new things.

But what you don't see:

- Overdue bills outside the frame
- Loans used to sustain the lifestyle
- The anxiety of not being able to stop

- Arguments about money

In other words, you're comparing yourself to someone else's display window without knowing the backstage.

It's the famous cost of looking rich.

How many people do you know who:

- Finance a phone over 24 months
- Buy "trendy" clothes and can't save $100
- Spend everything on the weekend and stay stressed the rest of the month
- Fear of the credit card bill, but refuse to stop showing off

They're buying status with their future.

They're trading safety for temporary validation.

That's a terrible deal.

Choose financial authenticity

You don't need to prove yourself.

You don't need to justify your choices.

You don't need to compete with anyone.

You need to:

- Sleep with peace
- Know where you're going
- Know that, step by step, you're building something real

And remember: the person who laughs last is the one who laughs with freedom.

People who plant with awareness don't need applause - they just need the harvest.

Simple strategies to protect yourself from comparison

1. Set personal financial goals.

When you have clear goals (buy a home, build an emergency fund, pay cash for a trip), it's easier to say no to useless spending.

2. Unfollow accounts that trigger you.

If an influencer makes you feel "less" because you don't have what they show, mute them. Protect your mind.

3. Celebrate small wins.

Saved $200? Paid off a debt? Cooked at home instead of ordering? Celebrate. You're building your freedom.

4. **Spend time with people who think like you.**

A supportive network with a healthy mindset strengthens your consistency.

Remember: it's not about what you show - it's about what you build. Your neighbor's grass may look greener, but maybe it's being watered with tears, maxed-out credit cards, and sleepless nights.

Take care of your garden. It may take time, but the harvest will be yours.

Your financial destiny is being built today

You may not have been born into money.

You may have made financial mistakes.

You may have been disorganized, lost opportunities, gone into debt.

But none of that defines where you're going.

Because your destiny isn't in the big events of the past -
it's being shaped now, in the small choices of the present.

Today you choose:

- Save or spend?
- Pay cash or finance?
- Plan or improvise?
- Give up or restart?

The most valuable minute is this one

Time doesn't charge you interest today.

It offers you opportunities. But it charges ruthless interest from those who postpone important decisions.

Every dollar you invest with awareness today can be worth ten, twenty, thirty dollars in the future. But every dollar wasted delays your dream by months, even years.

Think of the future as a road.

Each choice you make builds or break a piece of the asphalt, defining whether you'll walk it with safety or trip over the holes you dug.

Real life requires preparation and rewards discipline.

The economy will swing.

A job can end.

Health can fail.

Love can change.

The unexpected will knock on your door, and the only way to be ready for life is to take command of your finances.

And that command doesn't start with a bigger salary.

It starts with a smaller decision to act differently today.

You're building something even if you can't see it yet.

A healthy meal doesn't show results on the first plate.

A gym workout doesn't transform your body in the first week. Saving money for one month doesn't change the account. But repeat it for a year. Two. Ten. And you'll see that the small choice that looked insignificant became a new identity.

You won't just be saving.

You'll be building security, dignity, and independence.

You'll be teaching your children, honoring your story, and making peace with your future.

Success isn't what you do once in a while.

It's what you do consistently.

Small decisions, made with consistency, create big destinies.

Well-managed money is like clean water: it gives life, brings calm, and sustains roots.

People who live on impulse end up living in panic.

Your financial future is at stake.

You're already in the game.

You just need to decide which side will win.

From 7 days to 30 days

Now let's extend that 7-day challenge into a 30-day commitment.Write this sentence in your own handwriting:

"For the next 30 days, I will make at least one conscious financial decision per day.
It can be small, but it will be made with purpose."

Put that paper on the mirror.
On your computer.
On the refrigerator.
In your wallet.
Let it remind you that your destiny is in your hands.
You don't need to change everything.
You need to change today.

What looks small now will one day be your greatest source of pride. Because in the silence of consistency, financial freedom is built. Be steady, and stay steady.

You're planting greatness, even if it hasn't sprouted yet.
It's growing inside you.
And when it blooms, the world will see what you built in silence.

CHAPTER 20

Money in marriage, family, and inheritance

The hidden cost of expensive silence

Money conversations inside a family should be as normal as talking about travel plans, your kids' future, or Sunday lunch. But in many homes, money becomes a taboo, a minefield, something avoided as if talking about finances meant a lack of love.

That silence is expensive. Much more expensive than any card balance or late bill. Silence corrodes relationships, destroys trust, and blocks collective growth.

Most of us avoid talking about money with the people we love because of fear:

- Fear of sounding greedy
- Fear of sounding controlling
- Fear of judging or being judged
- Fear of exposing vulnerabilities (debt, mistakes, disorganization)
- Fear of touching emotional wounds

And often, we don't even know how to begin. What should be a natural conversation turns into a cold war of unspoken tension.

Love doesn't pay the bills, and love without dialogue gets expensive. A couple can love each other deeply and still destroy their finances. Parents can want the best for their children and still leave them lost without guidance. Love needs planning, transparency, and courage.

Money isn't the problem — what it represents is

For one person, money means safety. For another, freedom.

For another, control. For another, pleasure. For another, pain.

If you don't understand what money represents for each person in the house, harmony becomes nearly impossible. The partner who wants to save may look "stingy" to the partner who sees spending as affection. The parent who works nonstop may look "absent" to the family, even if their intention is protection.

Conversation starters that open doors without sounding like an accusation

Use questions that invite honesty. Listen more than you speak. Build emotional safety before you try to impose rules.

- *"I want to understand how we each see money. I'd really like to hear you."*
- *"If we had a financial plan together, what would be your top priority?"*
- *"Is there anything about money you avoid telling me because you're afraid of my reaction?"*
- *"If we're going to build something bigger, we need to talk about what we feel when it comes to money."*
- *"What did you learn about money growing up, and what do we want to teach our kids?"*

Start with simple agreements
(don't try to fix everything in one night)

Begin with basics and revise as you grow. Clarity reduces friction, and freedom only works when it comes to responsibility.

- *"We'll split bills like this: X and Y."*
- *"Any purchase above $X, we discuss beforehand."*
- *"We'll review our finances together once a month."*
- *"We want to save $X per month for our shared goal."*
- *"Each of us gets 'free money' to spend without guilt — within a defined limit."*

Couples can love each other and still be in different financial phases. One may be studying finance while the other avoids the topic. You don't win this with pressure — you win with example, patience, and invitations instead of accusations. Over time, disinterest becomes curiosity, curiosity becomes conversation, and conversation becomes construction.

Talking about money with the people you love is respect, maturity, and care. It's not control — it's trust.

Finances as a couple: an act of love that still needs a spreadsheet

Marriage is also a partnership. It includes affection, dreams, and care — but also bills, risks, responsibilities, and decisions. If you share a life, you should share financial awareness as well.

That doesn't mean everything must be split 50/50 or handled coldly. It means aligning expectations, defining roles, and agreeing on goals.

There's no single perfect model. What matters is that both people feel safe and respected, and that the model is reviewed as life changes.

Three models tend to work when there is dialogue:

- **All-in, fully shared**: income and expenses unified. Great for couples with stability, shared projects, and deep trust. Requires full transparency and maturity.
- **Separate accounts + a joint account for goals**: preserves autonomy and builds partnership. Often done by contributing a fixed percentage of income (e.g., 30% each) to the joint account; the rest stays personal.
- **Proportional split by income**: if one earns $3k and the other earns $6k, expenses can be split 1/3 and 2/3. Reduces emotional inequality and prevents resentment.

Common mistakes that quietly sabotage the couple

- Hiding debt or spending ("financial infidelity"): it erodes trust.
- Assuming the other person "handles everything": even if one is more organized, both must understand the basics.
- Letting the budget drift: not planning is the same as inviting chaos.
- Comparing your relationship to other couples: each household has its own reality.
- Pretending everything is fine to avoid conflict: today's silence becomes tomorrow's explosion.

Make a monthly "goals date"

- *"What are our short-, mid-, and long-term goals?"*
- *"What is each of us willing to do to reach them?"*
- *"What will we temporarily set aside together for something bigger?"*
- *"How much do we want to save per month?"*
- *"What reward will we celebrate when we hit the goal?"*

When a couple has clear and visible goals, even sacrifice becomes lighter.

Use technology as a bridge, not a trigger

Apps can help you track inflows/outflows, share goals visually, set bill reminders, and simulate savings or investments. But use the tools to create dialogue — not surveillance or tension.

And the kids? They're learning even when you say nothing

Even small children sense tension or harmony in the house. They learn about money far more from what they see than from what you lecture. A couple who plans together teaches that love and responsibility go together — that freedom comes with effort — that partnership is built.

Organizing finances as a couple doesn't kill romance. It protects it. When money is cared for, the relationship gains time, peace, and focus , and freedom to live what matters: love, family, and dreams.

Inheritance, succession, and legacy , without conflict

Inheritance is often pictured as property, cash, or valuables passed from parents to children. But there's more. Think of two layers:

Visible inheritance and invisible inheritance

- Visible inheritance: assets, real estate, investments, money — who receives what, how, when, and how everything is documented.
- Invisible inheritance: beliefs, habits, values, attitudes, and even traumas — the family's relationship with money, work, responsibility, and generosity.

If you ignore either layer, inheritance can generate frustrated expectations, sibling conflict, and a repetition of mistakes that took years to overcome.

Dialogue prevents surprises

One of the biggest mistakes families make is avoiding inheritance conversations while they can still be held with calm and clarity. When the topic is avoided, heirs don't know what to expect (creating anxiety and resentment), and assets may be left vulnerable due to missing documents, outdated beneficiaries, or lack of a will.

A practical legacy roadmap (start now)

Step 1 — Clear documentation

- Update a will or written declaration of last wishes (as applicable).
- Define who will administer the estate (executor/administrator).
- Ensure accounts, insurance policies, and investments have updated beneficiaries.
- If there is real estate, a business, or complex assets, explain the structure and next steps to the people involved.

Step 2 — Family transparency

- Meet with your spouse and/or heirs and present a simple "asset map": what exists, what's planned, and what can change.
- Talk about values: "What do we want this legacy to transmit?"
- Create periodic check-ins — something as simple as an annual "legacy lunch."

Step 3 — Prepare the heirs

- Teaching financial basics, responsibility, and values — awareness reduces the risk of future disputes.
- Include the next generation in relevant decisions to build consciousness, not entitlement.
- If appropriate, define conditions (e.g., adulthood, completing education, time in the workforce) for receiving certain assets.

Step 4 — Periodic review

- Life changes, and so does your estate. Revisit documents

every 2–3 years or after major changes (marriage, divorce, relocation, new business, etc.).

It's about more than money: it's about trust

A healthy legacy transmits work ethic, humility, cooperation, and long-term thinking. A poorly managed legacy transmits guilt, conflict, silence, regret, and emotional debt.

Do a 'conscious legacy' exercise today. Write answers you can revisit:

- *"What three values do I want my children or heirs to carry?"*
- *"What inheritance do I want to leave — visible and invisible?"*
- *"What documents must I organize (will, beneficiaries, list of assets) so my wishes are respected?"*
- *"Who can help me (attorney, accountant, trusted family member)?"*
- *"By what date will I review this (e.g., "By December 31 I'll hold a family meeting")?"*

Inheritance isn't "only for the elderly." Legacy is built continuously. If you start today, even with a simple document or a timid conversation, you plant clarity. What isn't spoken becomes legend, and legend becomes conflict.

Financial disparities inside the family: how to avoid silent wars

Every family is a mosaic. One sibling thrives early, another is still stabilizing. One relative lives modestly, another built wealth. The first truth: everyone has a different journey. Comparing outcomes without context is unfair.

Unspoken sentences become cracks: "He only made it because dad helped." "She pretends she's rich but lives in debt." "He could help more." Silence plus judgment turns into resentment.

Common friction points include:

- Different expectations (wanting equal contributions with unequal realities)
- No clear conversation about family expenses (events, emergencies, support for parents)

- Perceived injustice or favoritism (one sibling helped, another not; messy inheritance division)
- Financial pride or shame (fear of asking; shame of saying 'I can't')
- No clear boundaries (help vs. dependence vs. moral obligation)

How to handle differences with wisdom

- Don't assume: ask. "I want to understand how you see this. Can we talk respectfully?"
- Set financial boundaries. You can help, but you shouldn't erase yourself to satisfy unrealistic expectations. "I can't right now" is maturity, not selfishness.
- Respect each person's timing and process. Support can help, but respect is what preserves dignity.
- Never use help as power. Don't turn assistance into control or emotional debt.
- Be transparent in decisions that affect everyone financially (selling a family property, dividing inheritance, shared investments). No secrets.

Real-world examples and simple solutions

- Three siblings with elderly parents: one provided most caregiving and wanted recognition in the inheritance. Solution: a written agreement that acknowledges caregiving and sets a fair percentage.

- One child became financially successful while others struggle: solution: help as a gift, not an obligation, and set boundaries to avoid dependency.

- In-laws with very different budgets planning a celebration: solution: say it plainly: *"That amount is above my limit; I can participate within X."*

A gold sentence to keep in mind: Love without honesty is fragile. Money without clarity can destroy even blood ties.

Prepare the next generation (even if your assets are modest)

Teaching money is not a privilege of wealthy families: it's a universal need. Children absorb what they see, hear, and experience.

Even without leaving a large financial inheritance, you can leave a powerful invisible inheritance by doing things like:

- Explain your choices: when you save, invest, or decide not to buy, tell them why.
- Share responsibility: involve them in real decisions (vacation budget, grocery planning, saving goals).
- Build the habit of saving: even a small weekly amount creates a lifelong pattern.
- Talk about invisible wealth: honesty, work ethic, generosity, balance; many inherit money and lose it because they never inherited values.

Practical activities to start this week

- **Family Money Week**: once a week, 30 minutes to review spending, decisions, and goals together.
- **30-Day Challenge**: $1 a day — kids and adults save together, then review the result and what changed.
- **Stories of value:** share a personal money mistake and what you learned so the error becomes wisdom.
- **Legacy Mission:** ask, "If you could leave a legacy to the next generation, what would it be?" Write an answer together.

A widely cited rule of thumb says many family fortunes don't survive beyond one or two generations primarily due to lack of preparation and communication. Whether your estate is large or small, preparation is what makes a legacy durable.

Build a family culture of healthy finances while you're alive: a culture of conversation, respect, planning, and responsibility.

A simple equation:
values + planning + dialogue = a legacy that lasts.

Ask yourself: if I disappeared tomorrow, would my family know what to do? If the answer includes hesitation, secrets, or "they don't know," there is work to do — and you can start now.

Set a family meeting (even informal). List assets (even modest) and the values you want to pass forward. Create a yearly "legacy moment." Review annually. Celebrate progress.

Don't wait until you 'have more.' Begin with what you have. The value is in the habit. You're building more than accounts and assets: you're building trust, understanding, and freedom for the people you love.

CHAPTER 21

The status fallacy: buying what you don't need

When image becomes the new definition of success

"Have you ever felt an almost irresistible urge to buy something, not because you needed it, but because you imagined how you'd look, how people would see you, or how it would feel to be "up there" for a moment?"

Maybe it was a new phone, a designer outfit, a more expensive car than you planned, or a subtle upgrade, a pricier dinner just to post the glass.

Welcome to the status society, and its best-disguised lie: that looking successful matters more than actually being well.

It has never been easier to compare yourself and feel smaller than it is today. Social media magnifies pressure and turns curated moments into an unfair scoreboard.

Open Instagram or TikTok and you'll see:

- Friends at expensive restaurants, even if it's all in installments.
- Influencers displaying lifestyles funded by ads, sponsorships, or debt.
- Lives that look perfect, but are only the highlights people chose to show.

The cruel side effect is the fear of "falling behind." And that fear often pushes people into buying validation.

Purchased validation is a trap

When consumption becomes a shortcut to self-esteem, the risk is high. The boost fades fast:

- The shoes lose their magic in a few weeks.
- The new car becomes routine in a couple of months.
- The dream trip becomes a 12-month payment plan — and anxiety.

Then the bill arrives, followed by frustration: "Why did I do that? Why did I think this would make me feel better?"

Comfort vs. showing off

Let's be clear: there's nothing wrong with liking nice things. The problem begins when the desire to look good outruns financial responsibility.

- Comfort is buying something that fits your budget, has real utility, and brings genuine satisfaction.
- Showing off is when the focus is external validation, not internal value.

Ask yourself:

- *"Am I buying this because I want it, or because I want people to see it?"*
- *"Would I buy this if nobody would notice?"*
- *"Do I really want this, or do I want to look like someone who has it?"*

Simple questions can save your wallet and your peace.

What's behind the storefront is often insecurity

Many people don't buy from necessity; they buy from comparison — with a sibling, a colleague, a friend, or an influencer.

"If he can, why can't I?" "She's 30 and already bought a place — what am I doing?" "My friend showed up with a new car..."

Comparison fuels a race that never ends, because there will always be someone who has more, or seems to.

Your brain loves novelty, and that's part of the problem

Your brain is wired to enjoy novelty, reward, and conquest. Buying activates pleasure pathways.

But the cycle becomes dangerous: impulse purchase -> brief satisfaction -> emptiness returns -> another purchase -> debt -> guilt, anxiety, shame.

It's like using sugar to escape sadness: it works fast, and it charges interest later.

Many spending patterns begin in childhood

Some people who grew up with little try to "compensate" later with excess. Some who had everything develop dependence on validation through possessions. Some heard messages like "you'll only be someone if you have this," and carry pressure to buy status. And many who were never valued for who they are seek recognition through what they display.

These beliefs become emotional tracks that guide consumption without us noticing. The cycle breaks when we look inward.

Reprogram spending with intention : not guilt

This isn't about depriving yourself of everything. It's about learning to buy with intention instead of impulse.

You can like nice things, as long as it's pleasure, not fear. You can buy something expensive , as long as it's planned, not used to silence pain. Buy what you want. Just don't buy to look bigger than you are.

Exercise: The Desire Journal

For one week, write down:

- Everything you felt like buying (even if you didn't buy it).
- What triggered the desire (e.g., saw someone using it, felt insecure, wanted to change your day).
- How you felt before and after.

This reveals how and why you consume, and gives you your power of choice back.

Consumption is part of life. But consumption for appearance is what quietly corrodes you. When you see where your desires come from, you stop being a puppet of status and become the protagonist of your money, your time, and your life.

Build a financially healthy lifestyle without proving anything

"When you picture your "ideal lifestyle," what comes to mind — a bigger home, a luxury car, branded clothing, exotic travel?"

You need to learn to separate what you truly want from what you were told you should want.

Financial authenticity means coherence

Authenticity is not deprivation. It is coherence:

- Coherence between what you value (time, family, work, faith, leisure) and what you spend on.
- Coherence between your season of life (income, responsibilities, dreams) and your consumption standard.
- Coherence between what you show and what you can sustain emotionally.

When coherence is missing, the cost shows up as guilt, regret, anxiety, and eventually debt. Before adopting "the standard," ask: "***Does this reflect who I am — or who I was told I should be?"***

Comfort vs. ostentation (another angle)

- **Comfort:** a home that fits your family, a reliable car, occasional travel, spending on what truly brings joy.
- **Ostentation**: buying to show, maintaining expensive things to look a certain way, living under tension to cover the cost of appearances.

With comfort, you sleep well. With ostentation, you wake up worried.

Three lifestyle profiles that work

- **Value-Focused**: you spend on a few meaningful high-value experiences or items: rarely, intentionally, and within budget.
- **Purposeful Minimalist**: fewer possessions, more freedom; less debt, more options; more time and peace for what matters.

- **Conscious Growth**: you resist the "now" impulse to invest in "tomorrow": education, skills, business, independence.

You can mix these profiles. The key is choosing a style that matches you.

Practical rules that change behavior

- **Pause before buying**: if the amount is above your threshold, wait 48 hours. It eliminates most impulse regrets.
- **Define three spending levels:** (1) need, (2) conscious desire, (3) appearance/validation. Classify every purchase.
- **Create a "light-life fund**: money reserved for experiences that bring joy and that you don't need to show anyone.
- **Review your "mirror expenses"**: did I spend for myself or to receive approval from others?

Behavior becomes identity. That's how you change long-term. Protect yourself from social validation traps and aggressive marketing

Today's marketing doesn't just sell products: it sells identity. Not a car, but "the successful person who drives it." Not a bag, but "the elegant life." Consumption learned to speak to ego and emotional pain.

Here are simple shields:

- **Reverse curation**: follow accounts that inspire, not pressure. Mute what makes you feel smaller or more compulsive.
- **The 3-question rule**: before buying something you saw online, ask: (a) Does this serve me? (b) Would I have wanted it if I hadn't seen this post? (c) Am I buying from desire or influence?
- **The pause protocol**: when you feel urgency from an ad, wait 24 hours. If it still makes sense with clarity, fine — but most cravings fade.
- **Reinforce your real identity:** list achievements that aren't consumption: a course you completed, a hardship you overcame, a real friendship, a value you kept. Reconnect with who you are, not what you own.

Freedom isn't having everything, it's not needing everything

"Have you noticed how calm people with money don't need to prove anything?" They can buy, but choose not to. They prefer comfort over competition. They live at their pace, not at everyone else's pace.

True financial freedom is measured less in numbers and more in peace. Peace is what remains when you stop competing with people who aren't even watching you.

Align money with your real values

Ask yourself: "Has your money been serving your life, or feeding a wounded ego?" When money obeys vanity, it becomes a prison. When money answers your deepest values, it becomes a bridge to your goals.

Three steps:

- List your top 5 values (family, faith, peace, growth, freedom, health, yours).
- Look at your last month's statement and compare spending to values.
- Create a reorientation plan: redirect part of your resources toward what you truly believe.

Examples: if you value learning, cut the excess and invest in courses. If you value health, redirect spending on food, movement, and care. Coherence feels like liberation.

Radical authenticity is a quiet revolution

Everything changes the first time you say no to what everyone wants and you feel relief instead of guilt.

Often there's a 'contraction before expansion': discomfort before change, saying, "Not now," skipping a costly outing, feeling left out. But after a few months, something blooms: money left over the peace of sleeping without hidden bills, the pride of living by priorities.

In a world that competes to look successful, being real is revolutionary.

If you drive a paid-off older car, use an older phone without debt, enjoy a simple home dinner full of affection, and choose peace over appearances, you are not falling behind: you are arriving early: at freedom, awareness, and wisdom.

Remember an old saying: "Those who save, have." More than saving money, save something even more valuable discernment about what deserves space in your budget and your life.

You don't need the latest model. You don't need the trend. You don't need the place everyone talks about. You need purpose. You need peace. You need coherence.

The world will keep shouting for you to buy. Now you can answer, calmly: "Thanks , but I don't need that to feel complete." Because real wealth isn't what you display; it's what you carry inside, and when your money serves your essence, your life gets lighter.

CHAPTER 22

When is it time to ask for help?

The Silence That Pulls You Under, the Words That Save You

Have you ever found yourself lying awake, staring into the dark, replying to the question that won't stop pounding in your head: ***"How did I get to this point?"***

The credit card bill is already over the limit.

Your bank account is negative.

The rent is past due.

Bills are stacking up like rain on a leaking roof.

And then the fear shows up.

But worse than fear, pride shows up.

Pride is one of the biggest causes of silent ruin.

It's what keeps a drowning person from yelling for help, even when the life ring is within reach.

"Why is it so hard to ask for help?"

- Because we learned to connect personal worth to self-reliance.
- Because we fear judgment, rejection, and damage to our reputation.
- Because we think "asking" is lowering ourselves - when in reality, it is lifting ourselves.

A new way to see it: asking for help is wisdom

Asking for help is the opposite of weakness.

- It is knowing your limits.

- It is acting before the situation becomes a tragedy.
- It is moving forward when everything inside you wants to freeze.

**"Someone who asks for help isn't giving up.
They're getting back up."**

- *"How many marriages could have been saved if the couple had talked about money before everything exploded?"*
- *"How many businesses could have recovered if the owner had sought a consultant before going under?"*
- *"How many people could have avoided depression if they had stopped trying to look strong all the time?"*

The signs you should not ignore

Here are a few symptoms that it may be time to seek support:

- You feel anxious when you open your banking app.
- You keep paying one card with another.
- You can't sleep because of bills.
- You avoid people because of debts.
- You keep postponing financial decisions.
- You have lost control of spending, even while trying.
- You have tried on your own several times, and nothing changes.

If one or more of these signs is present, this chapter is your warning - and also your restart point. You can keep pretending everything is under control.

Or you can take a deep breath, look in the mirror, and say: "I don't have to go through this alone."

The right help, at the right time, can bring back hope, direction - and yes, even money.

"So, who can help?" Finding your sources of support

If you realize it is time to get help, the next step is just as important: knowing where to find that help, and choosing the right kind. Because not every conversation, every "tip," or every spreadsheet will solve it. You need the right person, at the right moment, with the right care.

- **A Financial Coach or Financial Educator**

This is ideal for someone who:

- Wants to organize finances but doesn't know where to start;
- Is in debt and needs a clear exit plan;
- Earns reasonably well but watches money "disappears" every month;
- Wants to learn to invest with safety and clarity.

What they do:

They help you build a realistic budget, organize expenses, plan goals, and create a personalized strategy.

Be careful:

Avoid "advisors" who only push products. Look for someone who teaches you how to think and decide, not someone who makes you dependent.

Practical tip:

In the U.S., consider credentials such as CFP® (Certified Financial Planner), AFC® (Accredited Financial Counselor), or a reputable fee-only planner. Ask for references if needed.

- **A Therapist (or a Financial Therapist)**

If your biggest struggle isn't just numbers but emotions, this is your path. It is ideal for someone who:

- Feel guilty when spending;
- Has compulsive buying (impulse spending);
- Grew up with limiting beliefs like "money is dirty" or "rich people are bad";
- Self-sabotages when things start going well;
- Lives in constant conflict with a spouse because of money.

What they do:

They help you identify and heal the emotional roots of financial behavior, rebuild beliefs, and work through self-worth and money-related trauma.

Sometimes what you need is not more control. It is more understanding of yourself.

- **An Accountant or Wealth/Tax Planner**

For those who have assets, a business, or multiple income streams and want to organize everything properly.

Ideal for:

- Retirement or financial independence planning;
- Taxes, investing, and estate planning;
- Safer structures to protect assets;
- Formalizing how assets will be divided in a family or partnership.

Often, preventing a legal or tax problem costs less than fixing it later.

- **A Mentor or Experienced Friend**

Sometimes it isn't a paid professional. It's someone with more road behind them than you.

Someone who:

- Has faced similar challenges;
- Shares your values;
- Is willing to listen without judging;
- Speaks hard truths with kindness.

A good mentor doesn't hand you a finished map - they help you draw your own.

Attention:

Don't confuse "free advice" with wisdom. Avoid following tips from someone who talks a lot but lives poorly. Not every well-intentioned person is prepared to guide your life.

How do you know what kind of help to seek?

Answer honestly:

- "Is my problem technical or emotional?"
- "Do I need knowledge or inner healing?"
- "What am I missing: education, direction, or courage?"

If it's hard to answer, start with someone who listens well.

Sometimes the best beginning is a conversation with someone who validates your pain and helps you see the next steps.

You don't need to know everything.

You don't need to carry it alone.

But you do need to take the first step.

And the first step can be a conversation.

An appointment.

A sincere request for help.

A message that says: ***"I'm ready to change. Can you help me?"***

Dignity in asking: dismantling the "I have to handle it" myth

I know there's an invisible weight behind the thought, "If I ask for help, it means I failed." But allow yourself to see it from another angle: Asking for help is not weakness - it's wisdom.

The myth of self-sufficiency

Since childhood, many of us were taught that the "strong" person is the one who handles everything alone.

That admitting need is weakness.

That showing vulnerability invites failure.

So, we let bills pile up, postpone conversations, and pretend we are fine. But this doesn't protect you - it slowly destroys you.

Many people avoid asking for help because they fear rejection, exposure, or looking "less than." Yet, many people around you are willing to help - if you can ask.

Vulnerability is not shame; it is growth

When you admit you need help, three important things happen:

- **You remember you are human.**

A human being who feels, who makes mistakes, who needs support.

- **You honor your dignity.**

Dignity is not hiding flaws. Dignity is facing them with integrity ,seeing what is wrong, acting, and learning.

- **You strengthen your network.**

At some point, everyone depends on others - friends, family, mentors. Honest requests often strengthen bonds, not break them.

When the load is too heavy to carry alone

Sometimes your financial problem is technical: "I need a plan." Sometimes it's emotional: "I'm afraid, guilty, or ashamed." Both deserve help. And the earlier you act, the smaller the damage.

If you feel:

- Anxiety when you open your statement;
- Trouble sleeping because of debt;
- You avoid talking about money or you hide bills;
- You noticed that pride keeps you from inviting help;

Then the warning light is on.
Don't wait for the alarm to explode.
Take the first step.

How to ask for help with dignity

- **Be honest:** "I'm going through a difficult season financially and I'd like to talk/learn/get support."
- **Be specific**: say what you need (planning, someone to listen, technical advice).
- **Choose the right moment**: preparing for the conversation keeps it from becoming only desperation.
- **Commit to action**: it's not only "help me." It's "I will act on what I learn."

- **Say thank you, and give back**: at some point you will help others too. That closes the cycle.

You are not "failing" because you need support.
You are training yourself to turn the scoreboard around.

From reflection to action: how to start seeking support

Now that we understand asking for help is strength, and we know possible sources of support, the question becomes:

"Where do I start?" Because knowing you need help and actually seeking it are very different things. Between the two is the abyss of procrastination.

The silent obstacle: the paralysis of shame

Many people know what they should do, but they don't do it.
Not for lack of intelligence - for fear of taking the first step.
That fear hides behind phrases like:

- *"I'll deal with it later."*
- *"This month is tight; next month I'll handle it."*
- *"It's not that serious; it will improve."*
- *"I don't have time right now."*
- *"I don't want to bother anyone."*

And days become weeks. Weeks become months. The hole gets deeper. Not because it was impossible - but because inertia won.

Action plan for anyone who wants to break the freeze

- **Make a commitment to yourself**

Take a piece of paper and write:

- ***"I commit to seeking help with my finances.***
- ***I will no longer postpone my peace.***
- ***Today my turn around begins."***

Signing it by hand carries real emotional weight. You are making something real that used to live only as intention.

- **Choose one form of help from the list above**

Go back to the options:

- FInancial coach/educator
- Therapist
- Mentor
- Accountant/tax professional
- A free or paid course
- A trusted friend

Choose one. Just one. Don't fall into the trap of trying to "understand everything first" before reaching out. Movement creates clarity - not the other way around.

- Book it for today

- If it's a professional, schedule the appointment.
- If it's a mentor or friend, send a message asking to talk.
- If it's a course, enroll.
- If it's reading, pick the material and start.

No vague promises. Action is commitment to change.

- **Prepare for the conversation**

Gather:

- Your bank statements from the last month;
- A list of debts (balances, interest rates, due dates);
- Monthly income;
- Fixed and variable expenses;
- Your expectations and goals.

This helps the other person understand you - and it forces you to face reality.

Write everything down and take at least ONE immediate action

After the conversation, commit to applying at least one thing within the next 24 hours. Fast action breaks procrastination and reinforces willpower.

"What if the first help doesn't work?"

Sometimes you see a professional and don't feel welcomed.

Or the conversation doesn't flow the way you expected.

Or the plan feels disconnected from your reality.

Don't quit.

Change the path, not the goal. Find another source. Learn what didn't work and keep moving. No help is wasted if you learned something.

Your financial future won't be built in one leap, but in one step at a time. And that step needs to start now.

You don't need all the answers - you just need to start asking the right questions, to the right people.

Turnaround stories: the power of asking and starting over

Maybe you still think your situation is too shameful. That asking for help will expose you. That nobody would understand. But the truth is, thousands of people have walked worse roads - and rebuilt.

Below are real stories (names changed) that represent many others. Stories of courage, pain, and victory.

Stories that prove: ***"The right help at the right time can change the direction of a life."***

- **Case 1** - The teacher buried in debt who found relief with a spreadsheet and someone who listened

Helena, 42, was a public school teacher.

She lived on overdraft, owed money on three credit cards, and cried at night. She hid her situation from her family and smiled at work, pretending everything was fine.

One day she saw a video about personal budgeting.

She tried to do it alone, but the shame was too heavy and the confusion was too much.

A friend introduced her to a financial educator at a community program. They sat down, organized every expense, and built a plan she could actually follow. The greatest relief wasn't the math. It was being heard without judgment.

Today Helena has paid everything off, and she teaches basic financial education to her students.

It all started with a request for help.

- **Case 2** - The small business owner who almost went under because of pride

Carlos, 37, owned a small sandwich shop. He was proud to say he "knew how to do the numbers."

Then the pandemic hit and sales fell by 80%.

He insisted he would figure it out.

He borrowed, renegotiated with suppliers, used every credit line, and still nothing. The debt only grew.

His wife suggested: "Let's talk to that consultant from the business association."

Carlos refused three times.

The fourth time, he went.

Head down - but he went.

The conversation was hard. The consultant showed him the business model was outdated.

But he also showed a path: adjusting the menu, improving digital ordering, renegotiating suppliers. Carlos implemented everything.

Two years later, the shop not only survived - but it also grew by 70%.

Today he says: ***"If I had asked for help six months earlier, I would have saved a lot of money - and a lot of sleepless nights."***

- **Case 3** - The young intern and the therapist who saved her future.

Rafaela, 24, was an administrative intern. She earned little but spent a lot. Her credit card was always maxed out, she owed friends, and she lived with constant anxiety. She kept telling herself she just needed more discipline. But every time stress hit, she shopped to feel relief.

It was not just a money issue; it was an emotional coping mechanism. A therapist helped her connect the pattern to insecurity and unmet needs.

She learned healthier ways to regulate emotions and built simple financial habits with support. She stopped living from crisis to crisis.

The biggest breakthrough was this: she stopped hating herself, and started understanding herself.

The pain you feel today can be the soil for your new beginning

Picture this for a moment: One year from now, you look back and say:

- *"I remember the day I decided to ask for help."*
- *"It was hard. It hurt. But that was where everything started to change."*
- *"Today I breathe better, sleep better, spend better. Not because I got rich, but because I took the wheel of my life."*

Nobody changes without facing the discomfort of admitting change is needed.

Nobody heals a wound by pretending it doesn't exist.

Dignity is refusing to give up on yourself

If you feel shame, insecurity, or fear of looking weak, remember:

- Weak is pretending everything is fine until you sink.
- Strong is looking yourself in the eyes and saying: "Enough. I deserve more."

Asking for help is courage.

It's you telling the world, and yourself - that you refuse to live a life of emotional, financial, and spiritual scarcity.

You are worth more.

You can do more.

And you do not have to do it alone.

Final invitation

If this chapter touched something inside you, do something now:

- Call someone you trust.

- Write the professional you have been rehearsing talking to.
- Share this chapter with someone who needs it too.
- Write down one concrete action for this week.

Because transformation does not live in ideas.
It lives in action.
A few sentences to carry with you:

"You don't have to be strong all the time. You only have to be truthful."
"Asking for help doesn't shrink you. It resets you."
"Even the wisest needed teachers. Even the wealthiest needed mentors."
"If life has brought you to your knees,
maybe it's so you can pray...
and stand up again."

My hope is this wasn't just another text.
May it be the green light you needed to turn the page.

- ***"I am going through something."***
- ***"I deserve to get out of it."***
- ***"I will ask for help."***

And above all: ***"I am no longer ashamed of being human."***
Your next step starts now.
And it will be lighter, because it will be shared.

CHAPTER 23

Fear of financial success

When Money Scares You More Than Not Having It

Have you ever noticed yourself doing everything right and then... stopping?"

"Have you felt that as soon as money starts to remain at the end of the month, an uneasiness kicks in?"

"Or that the moment an opportunity to earn more appears, something inside you hits the brakes?"

Some people fear poverty. But many people, and maybe you, fear success.

The fear you don't see, but you feel

At first it sounds strange.
"Who doesn't want more money, comfort, and freedom?
But fear of financial success doesn't scream.
It whispers.
It shows up subtly, almost invisibly. And yet it is there.

It can look like this:

- You start saving... and buy yourself an expensive "reward" right when the emergency fund begins to grow.
- You get promoted... and upgrade your lifestyle so fast that you stay in debt.
- You begin investing... and at the first bump, you pull everything out because you're afraid of "losing."
- You have a skill that could earn more... but you downplay it:

"It's not that big of a deal."

This has a name: financial self-sabotage. And it often comes from an unconscious fear of thriving.

Where that fear comes from

Nobody is born afraid of success.

This fear is learned.

And it usually comes from three sources:

- **Limiting beliefs from childhood**

Phrases like:

- *"Money changes people."*
- *"People with money are arrogant."*
- *"Rich people are all exploiters."*
- *"That's not for people like us."*
- *"Too much money brings problems."*

These phrases are seeds. If you heard them and absorbed them, you may have linked wealth to danger, loneliness, or guilt.

- **Unconscious loyalty to family**

It may sound strange, but it is real.

Many people fear earning more than their parents.

Or being the first in the family to achieve something.

It's as if prospering says: ***"I'm moving away from who I am. I'm betraying my roots."*** So, to "stay connected," the person unconsciously sabotages growth.

- **Trauma from previous losses**

If you have gained and lost before, you may decide not to gain again to avoid another loss.

"If I have a lot and lose it, it will hurt too much. Better not to have so much."

That quiet logic becomes a cage.

It turns success into a threat.

The cycle of guilt and punishment

Imagine you start to prosper:

- Your income improves,
- You save, you invest,
- Things are going well.

Then a voice shows up:

- *"Do I really deserve this?"*
- *"What if people think I'm full of myself?"*
- *"What if I lose it all and people laugh at me?"*
- *"Will my friends abandon me?"*

If you don't confront that voice, it will sabotage you.
And it does it in subtle ways:

- A purchase you "didn't need";
- A rushed decision;
- A project abandoned halfway;
- A choice that erases what you built.

And the strangest part? After you sabotage yourself, you feel relief. As if you say: *"Whew. I'm back to what's familiar."*

That's fear of success in action.

It drags you back to the comfort zone, even if that "comfort" is uncomfortable. Recognizing this fear is the first step to beating it.

Don't blame yourself. This fear is human.

Success comes with responsibility, change, and visibility. But it also comes with freedom, peace, and possibilities you deserve to live.

Limiting beliefs: the invisible chains that block your prosperity

Sometimes you do everything right - you study, work hard, save, and still feel something inside keeps pulling the brakes.

It may feel unfair. It may feel like the world is against you. But most of the time, what blocks you aren't out there? It's inside you.

Limiting beliefs are ideas planted over years, repeated by family and culture, that became "truths" without being questioned.

Like an unconscious program that says:

- *"People like me don't prosper."*
- *"If I get money, I'll lose it all."*
- *"Rich people are greedy."*
- *"Money is the root of all evil."*

Beliefs about money shape decisions. If your mind says, "I'll never be successful," your actions often follow that script - and opportunities get sabotaged.

Common beliefs that block success

- ***"I don't deserve to prosper."***

This usually comes from guilt or low self-worth.

You earn and invest, but deep down you feel like an impostor - so you give back what you're building.

- ***"If I have it, I'll lose it all."***

Sometimes you heard that growing up.

It becomes a false form of protection: "Better not to have than to risk losing." The result: you freeze your growth.

- ***"Prospering will push me away from people."***

If you grew up hearing that "whoever gets rich forgets their roots," you may fear losing the people you love.

- ***"Money is dirty - or it's for other people."***

"I'm a hands person, not a mind person."

"Luck has nothing to do with me."

That belief limits calling, investing, and growth.

- ***"I'll earn more, but I'll spend it all."***

You get a raise or a bonus, and a voice says, "Now I can."

Suddenly the raise disappears and the debt comes back - because the success was sabotaged.

How to cut those chains

- **A) Notice them**

Pay attention to your thoughts:

- *"What did I think when something good happened to me?"*
- *"How do I react when I see someone doing well financially?"*
- *"What phrases about money did I hear at home?"*

- **B) Challenge the belief**

Ask yourself:

- *"Is it absolutely true that I don't deserve it?"*
- *"Is there someone like me who prospered?"*
- *"If I could deserve it, what would I do differently?"*

- **C) Reprogram with affirmation plus action**

It isn't enough to repeat "I deserve to prosper."

Action has to follow thought.

Example: ***"I deserve to prosper because I work, contribute, and stay true to my values. Therefore, I will invest X% of my income into what builds my freedom."***

- **D) Surround yourself with evidence and examples**

Look for stories of people who came from where you are and still grew. The patterns are real: discipline, healthier beliefs, and a habit of learning.

The domino effect of changing a belief

When you change a core belief:

- Your identity shifts: from "I can't" to "I can."
- Your decisions change: you act like someone who can grow.
- Time starts working for you: you invest, accumulate, and build.
- Self-sabotage loses strength. You become your ally, not your enemy.

You can't out-earn what your limiting beliefs allow.

You deserve to free yourself from old beliefs.

They may have protected you once, but now they keep you grounded when you were made to rise.

Silent sabotage: how you can ruin your success right before you win

Fear of success isn't only failing to reach goals. It's a subtle inner movement that derails your path precisely when you're about to break through.

You start earning more.

You start saving.

You see real possibilities.

And then something changes:

- You buy something expensive because you "deserve it."
- You raise your lifestyle.
- Investing starts to feel "too small" for what it "should" be.
- You pull back. You stop. You get distracted.
- The plan stalls.
- Your finances return to "normal" - which was already uncomfortable.

That cycle is not random. It's sabotaging the future because the present became uncomfortably different.

Why does it happen?

- **Old identity vs. new reality**

You want to grow, but subconsciously believe that deserving something bigger breaks who you are.

If "I'm simple" or "my place is here," then prospering can feel like betrayal or displacement.

You wonder: ***"Who will I be in this new life?"***

That gap between identity and desire creates a freeze.

- **Fear of invisible consequences**

Success brings changes: responsibility, expectations, visibility, and maybe judgment. And if something goes wrong now?

For many people, fear of what comes after success is greater than fear of failure. So, self-preservation says: ***"Stay where you are."***

- **Guilt and the "right to victimhood"**

If you have identified your whole life with struggle and scarcity, success can feel like it takes away your identity as the one who "suffers."

Unconsciously you hold back: "If I'm okay, who will understand me? Who will admire me? Who will help me?"

So, success feels like isolation.

How to tell if you are sabotaging your own success

See if any of these signs sound familiar:

- When money increases, you quickly find a "valid excuse" to spend more.
- You see someone else's success and think, "I shouldn't earn more than them," or "I'd rather they earn it."
- When you are close to something big, you turn the goal into a reason to quit: "It wasn't for me," "too good to last," "it will cause problems."
- You suddenly avoid long-term plans, saying, "Let's just live for today."
- When you win, you feel discomfort, anxiety, or guilt instead of simple joy.

How to break the cycle and welcome success with wisdom

- A) **Accept that success can be natural - not dramatic**

Prospering doesn't have to be "too big."
It can be simple and sustainable.

- B) **Build a bridge between who you were and who you can become**

Don't abandon your story. Carry it with you.
"My past shaped me, but it doesn't define me."
That emotional transition matters.

- **C) Set identity goals, not only income goals**

Don't only think, "I want to earn X." Think, "I want to become the kind of person X allows me to be." For example: a present parent, a professional who leaves comfort, a person who gives generously.

Then success stops being a number and becomes purpose.

- **D) Create small proofs of success**

Start with modest wins: invest X each month, build a reserve, learn a new skill. Small wins strengthen confidence and reduce fear of the big leap.

- **E) Have a support system that legitimizes your new reality**

Talk with people who have been there. Read about sustainable success. Protect your emotional health - because prosperity involves mind, heart, and wallet.

Your fear of success may not vanish overnight. But you can learn to walk with it beside you without letting it drive.

"We don't abandon who we are when we grow. We grow to become who we truly are."

Success as a mission: turning fear into legacy

Ask yourself: *"If I succeeded, what would change for my life, my family, my community?"*

If that question brings anxiety or silence, the fear is still active. Because success often represents more than money. It represents mission, impact, and legacy.

Success requires posture - and posture can be scary

When you begin to succeed financially:

- Responsibility increases;
- Eyes turn toward you;
- Expectations change;
- The old standard no longer fits;
- You either lead, inspire... or hide.

If you don't feel ready to be the one who inspires, you may choose to stay where you are, even if you are not well.

You may not fear "having" as much as you fear "being different," "living up to it," "maintaining it."

The success that creates impact, and the self-protection that holds it back

Imagine you reach financial freedom. Then what?

- You can invest in causes, help others, and lead new projects.
- You might change environments.
- You might face criticism, envy, and pressure.
- You might feel guilty for "being elsewhere."

So, some people decide: "Better not to rise too high. Here people know me. Here I feel safe."

They limit success not because they can't - but because they fear what comes after.

From personal success to collective mission

Here is the turning point: Success doesn't have to be lonely.

It gains meaning when it becomes a bridge: to others, to values, to impact.

When you see money as a tool - not a trophy - something shifts:

- Fear stops controlling you;
- You feel part of something bigger;
- You act with generosity, vision, and legacy;
- The block dissolves because the small "me" becomes a larger "we."

Strategies to transform fear into mission

- **Redefine success**

Ask: "What is the true purpose of my success?"
Write: "My success serves to ______."
That shifts the focus from "how much" to "for whom."

- **Connect success to contribution**

Set aside part of your gains for something bigger: a cause, a project, a concrete act of help. When money serves others, ego calms down and mission strengthens.

- **Expand your identity**

The old you said: "I'm just..."
Now say: "I'm someone who..."

For example: "I create opportunities." "I leave a legacy."

- **Build visionary support networks**

Surround yourself with people who see farther, believe in you, and support you without envy. Success grows in an environment that celebrates, not cuts down.

- **Celebrate small wins consciously**

Don't wait for "the big event." Every extra dollar managed, every habit changed, every plan executed - these are wins. And wins create confidence for bigger success.

If you feel uneasy around "possible prosperity," don't attack yourself. That fear may be there because you are one step away from your bigger self.

The price of not growing: when staying put becomes expensive. You may think stagnation is "safe." But the biggest risk is not what you might lose - it's what you never become.

The bill nobody shows you

When you don't move forward, time doesn't stop - it charges interest.

- If you could have invested earlier, you lose years of compound growth.
- If you limit yourself, you may work decades just to pay the basics.
- If you avoid change, you miss opportunities that may never return.
- If you stay comfortable in discomfort, you avoid the leap that would bring quality of life.

Small decisions today compound over years - and the cost of not deciding becomes a debt you owe yourself.

"I'd rather not grow" - the sentence that costs a lot

Thoughts that keep people stuck:

- "If I rise too much, I'll be alone."

- "Maybe I don't deserve it."
- "If I'm powerful, people will expect more - I'd rather keep my level."
- "Growing now might pull me away from my roots."

Repeated, these thoughts become:

- Income below your potential;
- Spending driven by fear, not by a plan;
- Opportunities ignored or postponed;
- Guilt, anxiety, and a quiet survival pattern instead of prosperity.

Stagnation drains more than change

Compare:

- Scenario A: you decide to grow, invest, learn.
- Scenario B: you decide to stay "safe," without risk.

After 10 or 15 years, the difference won't be small. It will be substantial - in assets, life options, health, time, and freedom.

And if "not growing" becomes a legacy? You don't live only for you. You influence who comes after you.

When you limit yourself, you pass on messages like:

- "It's better to wait than to try."
- "Growing causes problems."
- "We keep what we have."
- "Wealth isn't for people like us."

Fear of success can travel through generations like an inheritance nobody chose.

How to calculate the invisible cost - and decide to act

- **Look at your 10- to 15-year goals.**
- **Ask:** "If I keep my current pattern, where will I be?
- **Quantify:** "If I had invested X per month instead of spending it on Y, where would I be today?"
- **Add the emotional cost:** peace, time with family, health, influence.
- **Decide:** "I will change something starting today."

The math of growth is real. Money you don't earn because of fear becomes a debt you owe yourself.

Fear of growth doesn't protect you from life.

It keeps you trapped in the life you once dreamed about.

Now you can decide: ***"I prefer the risk of trying over the weight of never knowing."***

Turning the tables: accept success and build with purpose

You have walked through these pages and named what blocks you. Now it is time for the final step of this stage: to accept that financial success is not only possible - it is desirable.

Not to show off, but to live with freedom.

Not to compete, but to serve.

Not to have more, but to do more.

When success stops being a threat and becomes a lever

Imagine:

- your income improves;
- your savings grow;
- your lifestyle rises - intentionally;
- you still sleep peacefully;
- you still keep your values;
- you are still you - just with more options.

That is not a distant fantasy.

It is the reality of the person who decides to stop self-sabotaging.

The plan: five practical steps

- **Define "success for me"**

Write what prosperity means to you, not to someone else.

It can be: "time with my children," "building a business that helps," "the ability to stop working when I choose."

- **Create sustainable milestones**

- Short term: save X per month.
- Medium term: invest Y per year.
- Long term: have the freedom to choose Z.

Each win reinforces the identity of the builder.

- **Celebrating without the need to show off**

A simple dinner, lunch with family, gratitude.
You don't have to post it.
You have to feel it. Mark it.

- **Share your success**

Tell the people who matter. Help who you can and leave space for those who will help you too. Generosity legitimizes success and reduces fear.

- **Revisit this journey every year**
- *"What changed in me?'*
- *"What did I think would be hard - and happened?"*
- *"Which belief limited me and I left behind?"*
- *"What is the next challenge that scares me - but I will embrace it?"*

Success is not an endpoint. It is a process.
It is construction.

- ***"Prospering isn't pride; it's justice toward yourself."***
- ***"Those who fear success are still trapped in scarcity."***
- ***"Your money is not a trophy; it's a bridge to a larger version of you."***
- ***"Growing with values is not disloyalty to your roots - it's gratitude with direction."***

Get ready. Because the next chapter will take us even higher:

"When success is no longer enough - what kind of freedom really matters?"

CHAPTER 24

Freedom is better than wealth

The Real Meaning of Financial Freedom

From an early age we hear sayings like "a penny saved is a penny earned" or "your money should work for you." But many people miss what those phrases are really pointing to: freedom. Not just wealth.

Wealth can become a cage: it demands maintenance, creates anxiety, and piles on obligations.

Freedom, on the other hand, gives you room to breathe.

Imagine having enough to pay your bills, take care of the people you love, live with dignity - and still choose what to do with your time. Not living on autopilot. Not living out of obligation.

That is not luxury. It is possibility. It is freedom.

When we talk about financial well-being, reputable research and practice consistently point to the same idea: it is less about the size of your balance and more about your ability to choose, feel secure, and reduce money-related stress. In other words, the goal is not to "be rich." The goal is to be free.

The difference between being rich and being free

Being rich often means:

- Lots of assets
- A high standard of living
- Visibility and status
- Constant maintenance of a lifestyle

Being free means:

- Choosing your path
- Having time
- Living with less pressure
- Enjoying what you have without needing to prove anything
- Owning your steps

Here is a line I repeat often: *"You don't need to accumulate to be free; you need to organize so you can choose."* Because if money is running your life - through bills, debt, or anxiety - you are not free, even if the numbers look impressive.

And if you have not accumulated much yet but you already control what you have, you are freer than you think.

Freedom in practice: what it gives you

When you reach real financial freedom, you gain:

- **Peace** - fewer nights trapped in worry
- **Flexibility** - you can say no to what drains you
- **Security** - you absorb shocks without panic
- **Dignity** - you live without begging life for permission
- **Purpose** - you can invest in what actually matters

The five pillars of financial freedom

Freedom is not built in one dramatic move. It is built through pillars. Think of them as a map - not only to get there, but to stay there with peace.

- **Pillar 1: Clarity**

Know exactly where you are and where you want to go. Freedom begins when you stop guessing.

- Track your income and expenses
- Name your priorities
- Define what "enough" means for your life

- **Pillar 2: Organization**

Organization is not perfection. It is visibility and routine.

- A simple budget that matches your reality
- Automatic bills and savings when possible
- A plan for irregular expenses (car repairs, insurance, holidays)

- **Pillar 3: Protection**

Freedom requires protection from shocks.

- An emergency fund (start small, build consistently)
- Insurance that fits your risks
- Avoiding financial landmines like high-interest revolving debt

- **Pillar 4: Mindset**

Your beliefs about money shape your behavior. If you don't accept freedom as part of your life, even when you have the resources, it slips away.

- " Do I believe I deserve stability?"
- " Do I sabotage progress when things start working?"
- " Who am I in prosperity?"

- **Pillar 5: Purpose and conscious choice**

This is the pillar that makes freedom alive.

- Money serves what matters: time, family, contribution
- You choose who you want to be, not just what you can buy
- You can say no to a job, a lifestyle, or other people's expectations

When freedom aligns with meaning, it becomes hard to shake. You are building more than wealth.You are building a life you can choose, not a life you are trapped inside.

Evidence and practice: what real-world research points to

When people talk about financial freedom, they want more than numbers. They want autonomy, clear choices, and less anxiety. Reputable research and practice align on a few concrete principles:

- Financial well-being is tied to feeling in control of day-to-day finances, being able to handle shocks, and having freedom of choice.
- Autonomy - the sense that "I can decide what I do with my money" - matters as much as income for many people.
- Consistent habits beat dramatic moves: planning, saving, and reducing high-cost debt are the boring steps that change lives.

A practical plan you can start today

If you want a clean starting point, do this:

1) Write down your real monthly income
(what actually enters your account).
2)List your fixed commitments
(housing, utilities, transportation, insurance).
3) Identify your "leaks" - the expenses that quietly grow
(apps, delivery, impulse buys).
4) Pick one debt to attack first (usually the highest interest,
or the smallest balance for momentum).
5) Build a starter emergency fund, even if it is $100 at first.
6) Choose one weekly money ritual:
15 minutes to check balances, bills, and next steps.

Reflection

Answer honestly:

- *"What would I do differently if I had real freedom?"*
- *"What am I currently doing that buys approval but steals peace?"*
- *"What is one small choice I can make this week that moves me toward freedom?"*

Freedom is not a trophy. It is a daily posture.
Organize, protect, and choose.
And remember: freedom is better than wealth.

CHAPTER 25

The wealth money can't buy

Invisible Assets: Far Beyond Your Bank Balance

When we talk about money, it is easy to stay on the surface: "How much do I have?" "How much do I earn?" "How much did I save?"

Those numbers matter. But the deepest value is not measured in digits - it is measured in what money allows you to be, feel, and give. True wealth is often invisible, and ironically, harder to build than any material asset.

" What does "invisible wealth" look like?"

Let yourself imagine:

- The peace of sleeping without financial panic, even if you are not a millionaire.
- A life with choices - time for the people you love and projects that matter - without needing to prove anything.
- The calm strength to say no when you want, and yes when it makes sense - not driven by social pressure.
- The ability to help others, not from guilt, but from real generosity.
- Self-respect: knowing you are worthy while you are still building, not just surviving.

None of that shows up neatly in a spreadsheet. Yet it shapes lives. And in the long run, it is what defines who is truly free.

Why experts keep warning us about this

Financial education is important, but knowledge alone is not the finish line. People also need capability, resilience, and emotional maturity around money.

That is why someone can earn a lot and still feel trapped - and someone else can earn less and still feel stable.

The invisible part is not mystical. It is built through decisions, boundaries, and values.

The main forms of wealth money cannot guarantee

- **1) Peace**

Peace is not the absence of problems. It is the presence of direction. It grows when you have a plan, when you reduce chaos, and when you stop living in financial denial.

- **2) Time**

Time is the asset you can never replace. Money can buy convenience, but it cannot buy back years.

One of the clearest signs of freedom is when your calendar is not owned by debt and desperation.

- **3) Relationships**

Many families do not break because of a lack of love - they break because of money stress, secrecy, and unresolved expectations.

Building financial clarity protects relationships: less blame, fewer explosions, more honesty.

- **4) Health**

Stress has a price. Anxiety drains energy, sleep, and focus. Money cannot replace health, but financial discipline can protect it by reducing constant worry.

- **5) Identity and self-worth**

If you only feel valuable when you are buying, showing, or impressing, you will always be at risk. Invisible wealth is when you know who you are even when your lifestyle is simple.

- **6) Character**

Money amplifies what is already inside. It can amplify generosity, or ego.

The richest people in spirit are often those who learned humility, discipline, and gratitude.

- **7) Legacy**

Legacy is not only what you leave. It is what you teach while you are still here. The habits, conversations, and values you pass on can be worth more than any inheritance.

How to build invisible wealth in real life

Try these practices:

- Keep your finances visible: a weekly check-in beats monthly panic.
- Spend with intention: ask "Does this purchase add peace or pressure?"
- Choose simple systems: automate bills, savings, and debt payments when possible.
- Protect your boundaries: avoid trying to fund other people's expectations.
- Practice generosity within your reality: giving is a muscle, not a performance.
- Invest in your mind: knowledge multiplies every dollar you earn.

A short exercise

Write down answers to these questions:

- "What do I want money to protect in my life?"
- "What kind of person do I become when I have more?"
- "What am I chasing that is actually emotional, not financial?"
- "What would enough look like if I stopped comparing myself to others?"

Here is the paradox: when you build the invisible wealth first -

peace, time, relationships, identity - money becomes a tool instead of a judge. And that is when you finally start living rich.

CHAPTER 26

Everything I learned (and I'm still learning)

When I Look Back, I See How Far We've Come

Writing this book was more than putting words on paper. It was a return to everything I lived, everything I learned, and especially everything I still work to apply day after day.

Across these pages, you walked through concepts, stories, exercises, and reflections that were not born in theory. They came from the field - from real life: meetings, overdue bills, late-night fears, and the kind of wins that bring tears of gratitude.

If you made it here, I could tell you something with confidence: you are not the same person you were at the beginning.

Not because you became a financial expert.

Not because you memorized the perfect percentages for spending, investing, or saving.

But because you understood something essential: money is a language - and you are becoming fluent in it, in the most human, realistic, and powerful way possible.

What we learned together

Trying to repeat everything we covered would be unfair - like trying to count the ocean with your fingers.

But some truths deserve to be said clearly, because they are the pillars of the new mindset you built:

- 1) A debit card is more than plastic - it is a symbol of control, presence, and reality.

- 2) Financial habits do not start in adulthood - they should be planted in childhood, with honest conversations.
- 3) A credit card can be an ally or a villain - it depends on who is in charge.
- 4) Renting is not always freedom, and buying is not always a prison. Context matters more than opinion.
- 5) Investing is not complicated - it is starting, repeating, and respecting time.
- 6) You are your greatest asset: your knowledge, your choices, your energy.
- 7) The economy is not distant - it is in your grocery cart, in interest rates, in the cost of borrowing.
- 8) We faced fear, guilt, and anxiety - and recognized them as part of the game, but no longer the boss.
- 9) We reflected on invisible wealth - the kind that doesn't show on a statement but saves marriages and builds legacies.

And the most important lesson:
you learned to see yourself as the protagonist.

You are no longer someone money drags around.
You are someone who leads it.
With awareness. With clarity.
With courage.

Learning never ends

And if I can be honest - as I have been from the beginning - here is a final secret: ***"I'm still learning too."***

Because life changes. The economy changes. You change.

Financial maturity is not a finish line; it is a practice. What matters is staying awake, staying humble, and staying consistent.

A 30-day commitment

If you want to turn this book into action, try this simple commitment:

- **Week 1**: Track everything. No judgment - only truth.

- **Week 2:** Choose one expense to cut and redirect that money to a reserve or debt payment.
- **Week 3**: Build one system (automatic bill pay, automatic savings, or a weekly money ritual).
- **Week 4**: Start investing in knowledge: one course, one book, one conversation that upgrades your thinking.

At the end of 30 days, write down what changed in you:

- *"What did I do that I thought I couldn't?"*
- *"What belief did I leave behind?"*
- *"What is the next challenge that scares me - and that I will embrace?"*

Final message

Reread what you need to reread. Highlight what speaks to you. Share what can help someone else.

And keep learning, because the person who understands money is always stronger than the person who only has money.

And here is the line I want you to carry with you:

**"It's not about how much you have,
but how well you understand what you have."**

See you on the next step.
With respect,
Luiz Birman

ooooooooooooooo

www.ingramcontent.com/pod-product-compliance
Lightning Source LLC
LaVergne TN
LVHW050911210926
848482LV00012B/399